Overdue Apologies

a middle school memoir
by Noriko Nakada

I never thought I'd become the kind of girl I became. It happened little by little, kind of like growing. You don't notice how tall you've gotten until your jeans hover several inches above your shoes. But that's how it happened. I woke up one day and hardly recognized myself: a stranger struggling to understand who I was.

Sixth Grade

Out

I walk across the empty playground under a perfect blue sky and head toward a low, red brick building. The first bell cleared the yard, so the bars and dodge ball courts sit empty. It's the first day of school, and for the first time I'll be the only Nakada at St. Francis Elementary. I thought I'd be more excited. Instead I'm nervous.

I pull open the door to a long, shiny hallway. A little girl sprints around me. Her bright pink backpack bobs down the length of the hall, and she disappears into the second grade classroom. I know what she will experience there. I know what third, fourth, and fifth grade will be like too. I had each of those teachers, and before me Chet, Laura, and Mitch did. The only room I haven't experienced is sixth grade. I enter through the propped-open door.

Many of my classmates have moved on to one of the two public middle schools in Bend. I do the math in my head: last year there were 29 of us, 11 are gone leaving 18 behind. The difference explains why the room feels so empty, too big for less than twenty of us. Loretta sits at a desk close to the door next to Faith. I smile, but she doesn't see me, or she's still ignoring me. Loretta and I have been friends since we rolled around on the floor as toddlers, but when Faith came to St. Francis in fourth grade things got complicated.

Mr. Roberts nods toward a desk in the front row, and I take my seat. I stare up at my new teacher and sort of listen to him. I smile in the right places and look up when he clears his throat. He does this before he asks a question that isn't rhetorical. I don't raise my hand.

I'm half-listening to Mr. Roberts, half-thinking about why Loretta didn't smile when he asks us to take out a piece of notebook paper. Please, don't ask us to write about what we did over summer vacation. Even if he did, I wouldn't have the words to explain any of it. I would push away the memories of what happened at home in the dusty silence of summer: all the confusion and worry. Instead, I'd write about Girl Scout Camp (and leave out how Loretta and Faith ignored me). I would write about swim meets and our cousins visiting from Los Angeles, but Mr. Roberts doesn't ask about our summer. He tells us to write about what we learned in the fifth grade and what we want to learn in sixth. We're just getting started when the bell rings for recess.

The playground blacktop radiates heat in the morning sun. Fourth and fifth grade boys play prison ball, and the sixth grade boys take over the basketball court. Loretta and Faith walk off by themselves making it clear: I am out. I figure this silent treatment is about Jennifer Douglass. I hung out with her last year when I was going with Jimmy Olson. But Jennifer, Jimmy, and my brother Mitch are all starting seventh grade at Pilot Butte today. I walk away from Loretta and Faith and I'm sure they're laughing because I'm alone. I head over to the basketball courts and shoot around with Rich Eiguren and Cody French.

For the rest of the day, I avoid looking at Loretta and Faith. I solve math problems: add, subtract, multiply, and divide. At lunch I sit with Karen Thornton, and we talk about swim team. During science, I imagine the vastness of the universe and the forever that is infinity. I watch the clock and count the seconds for the bell to ring on the worst first day of school ever.

When the final bell rings I walk outside and try not to cry. Mom is waiting. She doesn't look happy. She's probably been fighting traffic. I sit with a thud in the front seat, but Mom doesn't see me. It's just like the play we saw last spring, *Our Town*, where no one really looks at anyone. Mom doesn't notice I'm upset. She hasn't seen anyone but Chet lately. She has bigger things on her mind. I swallow hard and buckle my seat belt.

The station wagon speeds down Franklin, but after 100 yards we're stuck behind a long line of cars making their way to the east side of town.

"Are you sure you want to stay at St. Francis?" Mom asks. "You *could* go to Pilot Butte."

As the car creeps beneath the train tracks, I try to solve Mom's question like a mathematical equation.

The drive plus tuition at St. Francis equals a lot of money and an unhappy mom. If I'm not at St. Francis I can take away Mom fighting traffic, the cost of tuition, and Loretta and Faith ignoring me. Mom has given me the answer to the problem I didn't know how to solve.

"Okay," I answer casually. "I'll go to Pilot Butte."

Mom glances over at me. She tries to see me but my tears have dried and I've hidden away. That's how we do it in our family. We pretend there is nothing left to say. I stare at the brake lights and silently celebrate never having to go back to St. Francis again.

First Day: Take Two

The next morning, Mom drives Mitch and me to Pilot Butte Junior High. I brush off my new white Keds; smooth my Levis and baby blue polo. It's my first day of middle school, and I'm prepared. I've watched Chet and Laura transition to public school. I paid close attention to their clothes, shoes, and hair. Chet is popular. He wears badges for three sports on his letterman jacket and goes to homecoming and prom with pretty girls. Laura was popular in junior high but something happened in high school. The phone stopped ringing, and groups of giggly girls stopped coming to the house. Now she rarely gets asked to school dances and has only a few close girl friends. Still, with Chet and Laura as role models, I feel ready for my first day at public school.

Mom parks the station wagon beneath a stand of junipers, and the three of us walk toward the cluster of beige buildings in the shadow of Pilot Butte. The ponderosa pines, dusty from the dry summer, tower above the green grass at the front of the school. Mitch pulls open the door for us, wishes me luck, and heads off to his first period class. He had one day as the only Nakada at Pilot Butte. I bet he's disappointed I'm here, but he doesn't say anything. He pretends everything's okay. Even though Mitch is adopted, he's picked up the family habit.

We pretend our family is just like everyone else in Bend even though we're the only Japanese Americans in town. We pretend Dad is like every other dad even though when he was my age he and his whole family had to move to an internment camp in Wyoming. We pretend Mitch is just another one of us even though he's Korean and came to us when he was six. We pretend this past summer was only about swim meets and camp and not about the hospital or imaginary voices in Chet's head. We pretend things in the house on Jones Road are just fine.

I follow Mom to the main office and wait as she gives the secretary my information. The secretary says I'll be in Mrs. Gregory's class. I've never heard of her. At St. Francis, I knew every teacher, and every teacher knew I was the littlest Nakada, the end of our family line.

The secretary tells a student worker to walk me to class. As soon as I leave the office, I feel lighter. The weight of Loretta and Faith ignoring me lifts. Each step distances me from the worry hanging around our house. I subtract St. Francis, Loretta, Faith, and my problems at home. Pilot Butte is my escape.

We walk down the narrow sixth grade hallway and the student pulls open the door to my new classroom. A tall, thin woman with red, bushy hair stands at the front of the small room. Several rows of students stare as I wait. The teacher writes down my name. "How do you say...?"

I'm sure she's never seen a name like Noriko.

"It's Nori, just Nori."

She pulls a wadded up tissue from inside her sleeve, runs it under her nose, and then points toward an empty seat at the back of the room.

I feel everyone's eyes on me as I make my way toward my desk. Joe Speck sits in front of me. He nods but doesn't smile. Joe was in my class at St. Francis, and our moms are friends. He comes over to play with Mitch, and we've spent hours riding dirt bikes, jumping across irrigation ditches, and shooting hoops in the back yard. Joe's parents are going through a divorce, and he knows what happened at our house this summer, but we don't say a word to one another.

From the back of the room, I study my new classmates: a girl in front with short red hair raises her hand, a pretty blonde who already wears make-up glances at the clock, a boy in a hunting flannel stares out the window. Ten boys and thirteen girls equal endless possibilities.

Mrs. Gregory sets a few stapled sheets of paper on my desk: a multiple choice placement test. I leave the classroom and disappear into a world of words and numbers. I spend my first morning at Pilot Butte searching for the right answers.

At break, Pilot Butte casts a long shadow across the grass field. A group of boys toss around a football. Girls stand in clusters with arms wrapped tightly around their chests. I want to play football, but there aren't any girls on the field. My first decision: do I play with the boys like I did in elementary school, or do I stand here with the girls? Who am I going to be in middle school where people don't know I'm the youngest Nakada, play soccer and basketball, and get good grades?

As I watch the boys throwing the football, some girls from my new class introduce themselves. They ask about my elementary school, and I try to be friendly. The girls point out which guys are cute, but I've never heard of Dally Taylor, Gabe Sheerer, or Walker Stewart.

The boys set their sites on a whitewashed board with the center cut out. They take turns trying to throw a spiral through the middle. One of the taller boys, with a dark tan and black hair, takes aim. The ball ricochets through the hole and then bounces up the hill to where I'm standing. I pick up the ball, and the boys yell for me to throw it to one of them. I look up at the white board and line my fingers up on the football's laces. I cock my arm back and throw the ball for a strike right through the center of the board.

I instantly feel myself teetering along an invisible edge. Throwing that ball might not have been the right choice. I might have just shown them all up.

"Oooh," a couple of boys call, teasing their friends who hadn't been able to do what this girl just did.

I turn away from the boys, and shrug. The girls stare, but then the bell rings, so we walk toward the building. The boys follow, and someone yells, "Hey, that's Nori."

I look over my shoulder and sort through the faces. Cougar Caverhill. He went to St. Francis in second grade. I smile and wave.

"Nice throw," he says.

"Thanks," I say, but I try not to make a big deal out of it. If I want to fit in, I can't stand out.

It's only my first day at Pilot Butte, and I pray I haven't ruined things already. I have to pay attention and find the balance between standing out and fitting in. That will make all of the difference in junior high.

Math

Seventh and eighth graders at Pilot Butte switch classes each time the bell rings, but the sixth graders stay in the same room except for PE, when we go to the gym, and math, when we move to different rooms depending on our level. I stay with Mrs. Gregory for math, and a bunch of other kids come to our room.

"Nice throw the other day," a kid says as he sits next to me.

"Thanks." I try to place the tan face and dark hair.

"You're Nori, right?"

I look at him sideways. How does he know my name?

"Robert." He holds out his hand.

I almost shake it, but my palm is sweaty. I wipe my hand clean on my Levis before extending my hand.

Robert has older brothers and sisters who play against Chet and Laura in football and basketball. He's in Mr. Nelson's class. He asks what sports I play, and I tell him soccer and basketball. He challenges me to a game of one on one sometime.

"Sure," I say with a shrug.

We race through a series of fractions problems where we have to find the common denominator before adding or subtracting. I finish before him, but get two wrong. He finishes after me but gets 100%. I smile but hate that he did better than me.

For the rest of class we talk about which high school is better: Mountain View, where my brother and sister go, or Bend, where his family goes. Our future high school is not our common denominator, so instead we talk about the Trailblazers. In the opening minutes of sixth grade math Robert and I establish a playful banter. We find sports as our common denominator and become fast friends.

Morning

Every morning in the house on Jones Road we execute a carefully choreographed dance. Dad starts a fire in the woodstove, and Mom turns on the heater to take the chill off the rooms upstairs. Dad showers and leaves for work before the rest of us race through the shower. Mom makes breakfast and packs lunches. We scarf down pancakes, waffles, or cold cereal. Chet and Laura eat first, and then Mitch and me. We move near one another, through the kitchen, and around the breakfast table. It's a silent dance except for *Morning Edition* playing on the radio. We brush teeth, and then Chet and Laura rush out to the old Datsun 210 and drive to Mountain View. Mitch and I walk up to Pilot Butte, but not together.

Mornings in Bend are always cold. Even when the sky is clear, the sun's rays can't penetrate the cold of the high desert. In fall, yellow, brown, and red leaves litter the ground and the first snow paints the Cascades a gleaming white. Soon ice will form a slick crust along the roads. Every morning, I leave the quiet chaos of home and wait along the side of Jones Road to walk to school with Robin Crank.

Robin lives across the street with her new-age-mom, step-dad, and two sisters. Her mom buys organic chips and natural sodas. A couple summers ago Robin and I played makeovers with her Fresh 'N Fancy makeup kit, and when I came home wearing pink blush and blue eye shadow Laura said I looked like a clown. Robin has a tetherball pole in her backyard and an indoor pool where we play Marco Polo and Sharks and Minnows. Robin's older sister, Heather, is nothing like Laura. Heather wears thick black eyeliner and lipstick. She's into music and film. Laura never wears make-up, and she's into sports. Robin and I have way more in common than our older sisters, but since we went to different elementary schools we've never become close.

Once I start Pilot Butte though, I see another side of Robin. At school she is popular. She's tall and has an asymmetrical haircut streaked from the summer sun. She wears braces and so many cool clothes that she can go three or four weeks without repeating an outfit. Her best friend is Bianca Weston. Bianca and Robin went to Juniper Elementary together. Bianca is skinny with straight light brown hair. She lives in a huge house on Revere. Bianca has great clothes too and she doesn't repeat outfits forever. Kim Mitchell is their other friend. She went to Buckingham, and she's tiny (even shorter than me). She has shoulder length, wavy blonde hair, and she's a spaz.

I don't know how everyone knows in the first week of school, but already Robin, Bianca, and Kim are popular. Maybe it's the clothes and jewelry that only kids with money can afford, or where their dads work, or the size of their houses. I don't know exactly what it is, but the differences between the popular girls and the rest of us are clear.

Popular girls have Polo shirts, Guess jeans, Swatch watches, Trapper Keepers, rubber jelly bracelets, and Lip Smackers. Popular girls have a different attitude. They smile and laugh as they walk through the sixth grade hall. At lunch, they sit with the cool boys and ignore the rest of us. They are in the best class with teachers who are young and cool too.

Not-so-popular girls have Levis, hand-me down t-shirts, bare arms, plain blue three ring binders, and chapped lips. We walk nervously through the halls to our lockers. We grab brown bag lunches and sit with girls from lame teachers' classes.

Still, Robin waits for me every morning for the walk to school. Even though my family isn't rich, even though I don't wear exactly the right things or carry the right supplies, I think maybe, just maybe, I could be popular too.

As Robin and I walk down Jones Road, we leave behind the girls we are with our families and head toward the girls we are on our own. Clouds of breath appear and disappear before us as we talk about school, teachers, and mutual friends. Half way down the hill on Revere we stop at the two-story house with a circular driveway and a broad front porch.

Bianca's mom answers the door in her bathrobe. "Morning girls," she says sleepily as she lets us into the warm entry hall. The Weston's house always looks and smells clean. "Bink! Your friends are here," Mrs. Weston yells up the stairway. "Hurry up!" Then Mrs. Weston turns to us.

"Cute sweater, Robin."

"Thanks."

Robin and I look around the entry hall and wait.

"Sorry, guys," Bianca yells. "I'm almost ready."

"Your nails look nice," Mrs. Weston says holding my cold palm in her warm hand. She studies my fingers and the pale pink polish. "Where did you get them done?"

I've never had a manicure. "I did them myself," I say quietly, worried that doing your own nails isn't very cool.

"I wish I had the patience to do mine," Mrs. Weston says examining her French manicure and the red polish on her toes.

My mom files but never paints her nails.

Bianca rushes down the stairs, a messenger bag flung over her navy pea coat. Mrs. Weston looks her daughter up and down. "Your shoes don't match, Bink."

"Mom, they're fine. We're going to be late."

Sometimes Bianca makes it out the door, sometimes she sprints back upstairs to change. I walk with Robin and Bianca, the two most popular girls, up the path by the irrigation ditch toward school. We take our time, walk slowly, and I start to understand: If I want to be popular I have to be patient. It's totally not cool to want to be cool. I have to watch for a pattern and figure out what it takes to be popular.

New Friends

It's a Friday night, and Mom and Dad are going to see *The Gods Must Be Crazy* at Pat and Mike's Dinner Theatre downtown. Mom asks if I want to invite a friend. If I was still at St. Francis, still friends with Loretta, I would have called her, but now I go to Pilot Butte. I haven't done anything outside of school with anyone, but I have Jamie Richards' number from a project we worked on together, so I call to invite her.

Jamie wears thick glasses and has a quick smile. She went to Bear Creek Elementary and her best friend is Michelle Meteer. Jamie and Michelle are opposites. Jamie makes jokes. She flies through class assignments and talks fast. She raises her hand straight in the air when she has a question. Michelle is so quiet she practically disappears. If she wasn't Jamie's friend I never would have noticed her. Jamie and Michelle are in Mrs. Gregory's class with me, and I've been hanging out with them at break and lunch.

Jamie and I have lots in common even though it doesn't look like it. My dark hair, olive skin, and brown eyes are the opposite of Jamie's blonde hair, fair skin, and green eyes. But we're both extroverts, and we study people to figure them out.

Dad drives the station wagon to pick Jamie up at a small house just south of Greenwood, close to the 7-11. Jamie's mom walks out to meet my parents. I try not to be too embarrassed of our old car or my parents.

"Hi, I'm Jamie's mom, Melanie." Jamie's mom is young, and she reaches in the car to shake Mom's hand.

"Great to meet you, Melanie," Mom says and it's like I'm spying in on an adult world.

"What movie are you guys seeing?"

Mom says *The Gods Must Be Crazy*, and Melanie says she's heard of it.

"Well, have fun."

Jamie gives her mom a quick hug and a kiss on the cheek before climbing into the backseat.

"We should have her home a little after nine," Mom says with a smile and then we pull away.

On the drive downtown Mom lets us listen to Q94 instead of NPR. I'm nervous until Prince's "Raspberry Beret" comes on. Jamie and I sing along and laugh in the back seat.

After the movie we joke about the Coke bottle that fell from the sky and cluck our tongues like the Africans in the movie. I can't remember the last time I laughed so hard. We drop Jamie off, and she says she'll call me later.

Jamie calls on Sunday, and we talk for almost an hour about the movie, people at school, and our favorite songs from Rick Dees' Weekly Top 40. When I hang up I feel like, even though Jamie and Michelle are best friends, Jamie and I will be friends for a very long time.

Showers

The worst part of going to Pilot Butte is how after PE we have to take showers. Everyone says the two PE teachers are lesbians. They stand by the showers with their clipboards and make marks by our names as we rinse off. But that isn't the worst part about showering in the dim Pilot Butte locker room. The worst part is having to strip in front of all the other girls; hiding behind tiny dirty-pink towels that are so rough they feel like they'll tear your skin right off.

Some girls refuse to do it. They won't take a shower even though it hurts your grade. They girls hide out by their lockers while the rest of us rush in and out of the freezing cold water. At first I wonder if the PE teachers *are* lesbians, but after the first few times we shower I figure they're just doing their jobs.

I'm doing my math homework at the dining room table; waiting for Mom to come home from parent conference night. I finally hear the garage door open and Mom walks in. She sits across from me with a sigh, but she doesn't look at me. I can't imagine my teachers saying anything bad. I'm pretty sure I have straight A's.

"It was fine, Nori," Mom says. "It's just your PE teacher, Mrs. Holm, she told me I need to get you a bra."

My eyes go wide with shock, but Mom is embarrassed. She can't believe a teacher had to tell her this news; that she hadn't noticed the lumps pressing out from beneath my t-shirts. She's been thinking about Chet. All of her worry is caught up in him. I can forgive her for not noticing I need to start wearing a bra, but I'm creeped out by Mrs. Holm. I wonder if she wrote a note on her clipboard next to my name, "Needs bra."

Mom and I go bra shopping at JC Penney, but it doesn't feel like that training bra has anything to hold up. Now, every time I rush in and out of showers, I wonder what Mrs. Holm is looking at.

A Death in the Family

On a Tuesday night, a few weeks into the school year, I'm washing rice at the kitchen sink when Dad gets a phone call from Auntie Grace. She tells him their sister, Hannah, died of a heart attack.

I remember Auntie Hannah from *mochi tsuki* last year when we drove down to Los Angeles for New Year. Auntie Hannah helped Auntie Grace in the kitchen. She rolled balls of red beans that we wrapped inside the middle of warm, fresh-pounded rice.

"I guess I'll drive down on Friday for the service," Dad tells Mom. Money is always tight. There is no way we could afford a flight.

"Well, I can't leave the kids alone," Mom leans into the counter where she's battering up chicken to be fried. Even though Mom says *the kids* she really means she can't leave Chet. She is still hanging onto the weight of what happened this summer. "I worry about you driving by yourself, though."

"I'll be fine," Dad says as he walks into the utility room. He puts his work boots.

"I could go," I say.

Mom and Dad look at one another. I formulate my argument as I drain cloudy rice water from the bowl. Mom and Dad never let us miss school unless we have a fever or throw up, but Chet and Laura have football and volleyball, and Mitch sometimes struggles in school. I got a perfect first report card, so it makes sense for me to go.

"We'll talk about it later," Dad says as he heads out to the garden to pick vegetables for dinner.

That night Mom and Dad must talk it over because the next morning Mom says, "Let Mrs. Gregory know you'll be missing school Friday for a death in the family."

A death in the family. Most kids learn about death when a grandparent dies, but Dad's parents both died before I was born and Mom's are still living in Los Angeles. I didn't know Auntie Hannah very well, but *a death in the family* sounds serious. I tell Mrs. Gregory, and she says she's sorry. I don't know what to say back though. I'm not sure how I feel about a death in the family.

Dad and I leave before sunrise on Friday morning. We drive down Highway 97, past the dark small town storefronts of Bend and into the Deschutes National Forest. The sun rises and when we reach Interstate 5 I trace the sun's arch across the sky. I can't drive, so my job is to make sure Dad doesn't fall asleep at the wheel. Mom packed a cooler with snacks so we only stop for gas. Just after dark, we pull up to Uncle Yoshinau's house in Baldwin Hills. I sleep in the living room where I can see the Hollywood sign glowing in the dark and Auntie Suma and Uncle Yoshinau's tiny, white dog Sukoshi guards my feet.

The Nakadas meet at Forest Lawn the next morning. I hate that I have to wear a pink shirt. Even though I'm only eleven, I've been to funeral services before. When I was four Chet's best friend died right in front of him, and this past spring Bethy Hurley died from leukemia. I know you aren't supposed to wear pink to funerals.

Most of Dad's nine brothers are there with their wives and kids who are in college or older. Uncle George is missing. He died before Mom and Dad got married, and Uncle Sab isn't there because he never comes to family functions. I give Auntie Grace a hug and can't believe, with her sister gone, she's the only girl left.

Auntie Hannah's daughters, Susan and Ruthie are everyone's main concern. I don't know these cousins very well. I watch them and imagine how lonely it must feel when your mom dies. Dad and his sibling just lost their sister. I would be devastated if Laura died. I start to worry. With Auntie Hannah dying, death sneaks closer and closer.

My cousin, John, who usually cracks jokes all day, acts serious, and the easy smiles of my aunties, uncles, and cousins have fallen away. The sun shines bright, and the hot light hurts my eyes. In the heat of the afternoon men sweat through their shirts and women shed their heavy coats. We pray and I bow my head. There has been a death in the family but I never cry.

We eat lunch at a Chinese restaurant after the burial and I want to learn more about Auntie Hannah's life and the farm in Azusa. I want to hear stories about the war, about camp where Dad and the family moved after Pearl Harbor. I want to know about Uncle Henry and Uncle Sab in the 442nd, and Uncle Min and Uncle Yoshinau in Special Forces. I hope someone will mention Uncle George's death, which is only whispered about. I want to know why Uncle Sab isn't here: why he never comes to family gatherings. I hear none of these stories, and Dad wants to get on the road. Auntie Grace thinks we should wait; get some sleep, leave in the morning, but Dad wants to get home in time for Sunday mass.

The sun drops as we head out of the city and I don't know Auntie Hannah any more than I did before. Dad focuses on the road as the city rushes past my window.

"I'm glad you came with me, Noriko," he says.

I wish I could record Dad saying my name. He's the only one who calls me Noriko and pronounces it perfectly. I can't even say my own name properly.

"I'm glad I did too, Dad," I say and then the silence of the road settles around us as LA becomes a distant glow in the rear-view mirror.

Dad's face gleams from the darkness and I want him to tell me stories about Auntie Hannah. Dad rarely mentions his younger sister, what she was like as a little girl, or a woman, a wife and a mother. I want to hear about Uncle George, too. Why did he kill himself? Why don't we ever see his kids or his ex-wife? Uncle George is a family mystery, a secret. He is one of the things the Nakadas don't talk about: the war, the camps, their parents, George, and Sab. I wonder if Auntie Hannah will be added to that list.

As we enter Oregon I wonder how Chet, Laura, Mitch, and I will talk about our family history. What will happen to the story of this past summer? Maybe we'll talk about the Striegels' visit or the puppy I kept for two weeks. Will we ever talk about the voices in Chet's head and his hospitalization, or will we inherit the silence of our parents?

I stay awake through the night and ask Dad how he's doing. He says he's fine, but he occasionally opens the window to let in a rush of cold air. He tells no stories of growing up, or of life in LA before he and Mom moved to Oregon. I make sure Dad is awake but don't ask any of the questions swirling in my mind.

Dad grips the wheel as snowflakes drift down from the dark sky. The road before us turns from black to white and the muscles in his forearms flex taut. I can't sleep even though I'm exhausted and Dad mentions how glad he is Mom isn't here. "She hates driving in the snow."

I nod in the darkness, mesmerized by the flakes dancing in the headlights. Dad and I hardly speak as the green markers along the side of the highway tick off the miles.

Dawn breaks as we enter the familiar streets of Bend. The hot sun from the memorial service and the lives of the Nakadas seem further than a thousand miles away. By the time we pull into the driveway of our house on Jones Road the world has turned white. Winter's first snow buries dead leaves, brown grass, and all of our family secrets.

Touchdown Nakada

I love being the only Nakada to have gone to sixth grade at Pilot Butte. At St. Francis I was the littlest Nakada, and I hardly knew who I was outside of the shadows of my older brothers and sister stretching over me.

"Just wait until next year," Mitch tells me. "All of the seventh grade teachers know Chet and Laura, and they'll know me too. You'll just be one more Nakada."

But this year, in the sixth grade hall, no one knows my siblings. Robert White knows about Chet and Laura's athletic accomplishments, but only Joe Speck knows my family. In the sixth grade hall I can be silly and smart without comparisons to Mitch, who is so friendly, or Laura, who is quiet in class but aggressive on the court, or Chet, the three-sport athlete with a near 4.0 GPA.

In the sixth grade hall I am Nori who went to St. Francis and started late, who drove down to California because of a death in the family, who has Mrs. Gregory, and is in the high math class, who the teachers chose to give the welcome speech at Back to School Night, who hangs out with Jamie and Michelle, and walks to school with Robin and Bianca.

No one knows the secrets I hold. No one knows how this summer Chet came home from Young Life Camp talking too fast and wearing a too-wide smile; how his eyes couldn't focus for longer than a second. I've never told anyone I snuck into Chet's room with a tape recorder to find out if he was on drugs or had gotten some girl pregnant. I only recorded static and U2 blaring on his stereo, but two days later Chet was gone leaving Laura, Mitch, and I to navigate a sea of confusion on our own. No one needs to know any of that in the freedom of the sixth grade hall.

In November, the Mountain View football team makes it to the state quarterfinals. The family hasn't missed a single game of Chet's senior year, but it's not just because the team is good or because Chet will be leaving for college soon. Our family doesn't watch number 24 because he's the smallest cornerback on the team and a mistake could cost the team a touchdown. We watch Chet because we almost lost him to voices we couldn't hear, to a weeklong hospital stay, and to meds that help him sleep and keep voices at bay. We watch number 24 for a glimpse of the carefree smile, or the up-to-no-good grin we used to catch in pictures, but that he couldn't muster for any of his senior portraits.

The game is at the Civic Center in Portland, and Dad puts snow tires on the station wagon for the drive over the pass. A cold front brings freezing rain that covers the field with ice. The teams can't move the ball in the slick surface. Mountain View ends up down 2-0 after a safety.

Late in the fourth quarter Gresham makes a drive that stalls around the Mountain View 30. They elect to punt and number 24 falls back to receive. My hands are so cold I can't imagine catching a football with my frozen fingers, but Chet fields the ball cleanly. He cuts to the edge and sprints up the sideline. I scan the blue uniforms to see if anyone can catch him, but ice is the only thing between Chet and the end zone.

By the time Chet slides across the frozen turf for the touchdown the whole crowd is on its feet. Laura cheers with the band and fans hug Mom and Dad. I look for Chet in the swarm of teammates pummeling him, but Mountain View is back on defense so number 24 makes his way back on the field for the game's final minutes.

Time expires and Mountain View wins. Chet looks up into the crowd. He spots us and waves, revealing a smile we've missed, a smile that shines all the way from the field.

Chet makes the highlight reel on the local news and the Bend Bulletin runs a picture of my brother skating across the ice with the headline: Nakada Carries Cougs at State. When I show up to school on Monday classmates who never talked to me before ask if I'm related to Chet Nakada. Jamie, who already thought Chet was cute, is even more enamored. People who don't follow football know about Mountain View's big win and my brother's touchdown run. Over the course of a single weekend everyone finds out I'm just another Nakada.

Chet Nakada becomes the kid who scored the winning playoff touchdown, a small town sports star. There isn't room in this story for the trouble Chet faced this summer. Laura, Mitch, and I, who have always been Chet's younger siblings, watch Chet raise the bar on us again. Chet casts a long shadow Laura, Mitch, and I measure ourselves against and with the spotlight shining more brightly than ever, we fade away into the background.

Barry Anniversary

A week after we come back from winter break I miss another couple days of school for Grandma and Grandpa Barry's 50th wedding anniversary. Mom's parents are the only grandparents I know, and fifty years is a long time, so we all get to miss school and Chet and Laura miss basketball games for us party in LA.

The car feels crowded compared to when Dad and I drove down for Auntie Hannah's service. I have every mile of the long drive memorized from our last trip, but when we get off the freeway in the valley instead of driving into the city to Baldwin Hills I remember that Mom and Dad's families live in completely different parts of the same city.

We stay at Aunt Bev's house where the TV is always on and it smells like two things we never have at our house: alcohol and cigarettes. Laura and I stay in Traci's room where she's plastered pictures from *Teen Beat* on the walls and keeps her door closed to keep out the cigarette smoke.

On Saturday afternoon we dress up. I wear the same gray skirt I wore to Auntie Hannah's funeral with a blue and white striped oxford, tights and flats. Laura wears a red and black dress, and Chet and Mitch wear slacks, oxfords, and sweaters. We look so preppy compared to our cousins who don't dress up at all.

We walk into a Catholic church in Burbank where Great Aunt Marian goes to mass regularly. Our aunts and cousins don't go to mass so we're the only ones who genuflect and make the sign of the cross. The church is way bigger than St. Francis, but even with Great Aunt Marian and her family there we only fill the front two pews on the left side of the church. I've never been in this church before, but it feels like a familiar friend. Since leaving St. Francis I don't go to mass twice a week, and I miss the routine of sitting, kneeling, standing, and praying. But this service isn't a mass. Today Grandma and Grandpa stand before the priest and he blesses their marriage.

After the ceremony we drive to a restaurant high on a hill. Our cousin Michelle meets us there and she looks like she could be friends with Molly Ringwald with her silk pink blazer, silver bangles, and hoop earrings. Chet, Laura, Mitch, and I look so small-town compared to her. I wonder what Laura thinks since she and Michelle are the same age. Michelle looks five years older, though, with her make-up and cool clothes. Laura doesn't say anything. None of us mention how hard it is to believe these cousins, with their blonde hair and light eyes, are related to us at all.

I sit at the end of a long table in front of a huge window and watch the sun set over the valley. Our cousins spend more time with Grandma and Grandpa than we do, so as they talk and joke I feel like an outsider. I ignore Grandpa's comments about Mexicans and Blacks and wonder what he thinks of all of us with our dark hair and olive skin. I envy Traci's blonde hair and Michelle's short asymmetrical cut. I wish I could erase my Japanese traits and our small-town life. I try to feel proud that we play sports, get good grades, and go to church every week, but I'm embarrassed that the Nakadas are so different from the rest of Mom's family.

After dinner we walk outside and I stare at the lights scattered across the valley like diamonds. The streetlights twinkle and the stars in the sky seem so dim. I feel every mile that separates me from LA and try to solve the equation for why I feel so alone even with all of these people surrounding me. It's too big, though. I can't do the math in my head to find the sum of all the miles and all our differences.

I open the door to our family's station and wait for everyone else to say their goodbyes. I can't wait to get back to the frozen world of Bend, to escape the bright lights of this sprawling city, and bury how foreign our California family makes me feel.

In

On a winter morning when spring still feels months away, Robin, Bianca, and I make our way to school. Bianca asks about my weekend and I tell her it was boring. I ask about hers and she and Robin tell me about a project they have to present. I wish them luck as they disappear into their classroom. Jamie waits at my locker to tell me Dally Taylor smiled at her. I roll my eyes, but she's still looking down the hall so she doesn't see. As the two of us walk toward Mrs. Gregory's classroom I realize I'm happy.

I'm glad to be at Pilot Butte. I would have been miserable if I was still at St. Francis and being away from my family is such a relief. Chet's still on anti-depressants and Laura has a stress fracture in her foot and could probably use some anti-depressants herself. Mom and Dad have started couples therapy. Mitch and I are adjusting to our new school, but that isn't such a big deal, not compared to all of the other ways our family is broken. At school I'm allowed to be happy. I don't have to worry about how everyone else feels or check for signs of someone going crazy. If I had to choose between family and school, Pilot Butte definitely wins.

In this new contentment, I arrive at a conclusion. I've studied the situation at Pilot Butte long enough. I've been patient. I've watched the sixth, seventh, and eighth graders. I've made new friends, and I think I have enough of the variables figured out to try something new.

At lunch, I start out sitting with Jamie and Michelle like usual eating my brown bag lunch. I scan the cafeteria and notice Niko and Lance (the coolest eighth graders) hanging out by the stage. I glance at Robert and his friends. I see Mitch sitting with the cool seventh graders (not sure how that happened). I watch the popular sixth grade table from my peripheral vision like I've done every day for months. Robin and Bianca sit next to one another, Kim across from them, and

Ezra and Gabe next to Kim. One side of their table is practically empty.

Half way through lunch I tell Jamie and Michelle I'm going over to say hi. I walk over and slide along the empty side of the table by Robin and Bianca. I ask them how their presentation went and they laugh. Robin tells me it was a disaster. I pay close attention to looks exchanged around the table. I don't talk to any of the boys or to Kim. We've never been introduced, so even though I know who they are, I have to play it cool. After a minute I walk away, make my way back to my table as if it is the most normal thing in the world to walk across the cafeteria to talk to the cool table.

For the next couple of weeks I find reasons to talk with Robin and Bianca, but some days I don't talk to them at all. At the end of the second week Bianca introduces me to Kim and we say hi.

One morning on the walk to school, Robin turns to me. "Why don't you sit at our table at lunch?"

I look at Bianca and wonder if the two of them have discussed this. She shrugs. "Yeah, why not?"

"Well, I don't want to ditch Jamie and Michelle," I say casually. I know it's risky to pull my new friends along with me.

"They can sit with us too," Robin says.

I shrug my shoulders. "Okay, cool." I act like it's nothing but this is huge. When we get to school Robin and Bianca head to their class. I walk to my locker in the middle of D Hall and look for Jamie and Michelle. I can't wait to tell them the news. We're in.

That day at lunch, Jamie and Michelle are hesitant, but they come with me to sit at the cool table. I found the algorithm that has put us alongside Robin, Bianca and Kim. We meet Gabe and Ezra and I realize the next problem already whirling around in my mind is once you're cool, how do you stay cool?

Now that I'm in, I don't just walk to school with Bianca and Robin. Now they wait for me after school and we walk home together. Sometimes Bianca walks to Robin's house and we all hang out.

One Friday afternoon Kim joins us too because she's staying the night at Robin's. I don't know Kim very well, but that day I learn she and her step-dad don't get along, she went to Buckingham Elementary with Gabe and remembers when he had to wear a helmet to school for a medical condition. Kim pours Nerds into her mouth, and she walks faster than Robin and I usually do. Kim is hyper. "I ate like three boxes of Nerds," she says, laughing. Robin and I shake our heads.

Once we're at Robin's house we watch *Days of Our Lives*. We study the drama of Bo and Hope, Kayla and Patch, and John and Marlena with more intensity than any homework. We drink natural sodas and slide across the hardwood floors in our socks. We blast The Pet Shop Boys from the tape deck and sing "West End Girls" and "What Have I Done to Deserve This?" Then it's Human League, "Don't, don't you want me?"

When Robin's sister gets home from high school we giggle and jump onto the couch as she stomps past us in her long black skirt, black boots, black shirt, and black lipstick. We imagine just how much she hates us as she disappears into her room.

Around 5:00, I walk home for dinner. Dusk settles in and I know the time between school and home, those minutes I spend walking and hanging out, might be the most important moments for staying popular.

Family or Friends

One night, Chet and Laura don't have basketball games so Mom plates salad, lasagna, and garlic bread for dinner. In the quiet of dinner, I ask Mom if I can hang out at Bianca's after school.

"Bianca? What kind of name is that?" asks Chet.

"It's Bianca Weston's name, that's who," I say, annoyed.

"Weston? The Westons with the big house on Revere? You're going over there?" Laura asks.

Chet laughs. "You know her dad pulled a rifle on us?"

Family legend goes that when we lived on Shepard Road Chet, Laura, and Ray and June Garretson used to walk home from the bus stop and take a short cut through the Weston's yard. It cut about a half-mile off their walk, but Mr. Weston saw this as trespassing and warned them to stay off his property. They took to crawling through the dry irrigation ditch in winter in order to sneak past the Weston's house. One afternoon, though, Mr. Weston stood in the second story window and waved his rifle at them. That was enough to keep them from cutting through the yard again.

"Well, that's Mr. Weston," I say. "Bianca's not like that." I haven't even met Mr. Weston. He runs a Tavern and isn't home much.

Chet shrugs, Laura continues eating her lasagna, and Mom says it's fine if I go to Bianca's after school. I pick at my salad and pretend not to care what Chet and Laura think. My world at Pilot Butte is way more important than dinner conversation in the house on Jones Road. I glare at my plate to avoid looking at Dad, Mom, Chet, Laura, or Mitch. I care more about my friends than this family. I finish eating and ask to be excused. I push away from the table and hate my family. I hate them for judging me, for judging my friends. I keep my hatred hidden away, though. I pretend everything is fine as I turn and walk away.

Challenger

It's a cold Tuesday morning in Mrs. Gregory's class. I watch the clock and count the seconds to break. I'd hoped we'd get to watch the Space Shuttle launch, but instead we're writing about what the teacher aboard the Challenger should teach her students when she gets back from outer space. I wonder how Christie McCullough was chosen to fly into space instead of Mrs. Gregory.

I write about how she should describe floating in zero gravity. Mrs. Gregory steps out into the hall. When she comes back her hands shake. The tissue she keeps stuffed up her sleeve trembles as she shields her face and mumbles, "They're gone. The Space Shuttle exploded."

I let out a laugh. Maybe it's because I'm not sure how to react to Mrs. Gregory's shaking and tears, but I glance around the classroom and correct myself immediately. My laughter was completely wrong. I peer over my shoulder and feign shock because my classmates all look confused and concerned. Their responses are appropriate. I don't know what made me laugh.

It's all over the news and as the nation mourns I try to justify my response. I have the math of tens of thousands killed in Hiroshima and Nagasaki in my mind. I have images of priests, nuns, and the disappeared piled in open graves by Salvadoran death squads. These numbers overwhelm the seven aboard the doomed Space Shuttle. The Cold War, the nuclear arms race, and the devastation of my brother's battle with voices seem more real than white streaks falling through a cold winter sky.

But if I think about the families of the seven astronauts aboard the Challenger, I feel a sense of grief. I remember when Chet's best friend died and our whole house felt like it sank underwater, and when Bethy Hurley lost her fight with cancer and all of the color washed out of her family's faces. I think of Auntie Hannah and her daughters, left without a mother. I imagine the families of the astronauts sitting at home where it's too quiet and no one knows what to say. I calibrate my response to match everyone else's. I'm sad and when people talk about it I say, "It's so awful." I don't mention to anyone that when I first heard about the Space Shuttle Challenger, I laughed.

Boys

After a few weeks at the cool table I learn that a key variable to being popular is a boy liking you. It's best if a popular boy likes you, even better if a popular seventh or eighth grade boy does, but any boy helps. It doesn't even matter if you like them back. I hear Walker Stuart likes me. He's cute, but I only think of him as a friend. Still, it helps my popularity.

I have two older brothers and know boys from soccer and Little League, but in middle school things change between boys and girls. I don't play with them during break or at lunch, and when it comes to going out or dating, my older brothers and sisters don't help. Chet takes girls to homecoming and prom, but he never has a girlfriend. Laura only goes to dances if she gets asked, and Mitch never asks girls out. I have to figure out boys on my own.

Gabe is the most popular sixth grade boy. He goes out with seventh grade girls and is the tallest sixth grade boy. He hangs out with Ezra who has blonde hair and looks like a surfer. Even though I'm friends with a lot of sixth grade boys, I don't *like* any of them. I think the eighth grade boys are cute and Niko Gonzales and Lance Dillard are cutest. They're skaters and write for the school newspaper. Whenever the paper comes out I study the columns about what's hot and what's not. I make sure I'm not parting my hair on the wrong side or wearing the same outfit two days in a row.

There's a picture of Niko skating one issue and he looks like Ralph Macchio from *The Karate Kid*. When I see him in the eighth grade hallway or on the path between classes, my face turns hot. I can't speak. I plan what I'll say the next time I see him. I'll wave, smile and say hi. Maybe I'll even walk through the eighth grade hall. Next time I'll say something. Next time for sure.

In Bend, you go to one of the two middle schools: Cascade, on the west end of town, or Pilot Butte. One weekend, Bianca has a party and she invites kids from Cascade: Ryan Combs, Duffy Bryant, Jeff Burton, and Peter Moore. They wear matching red and black North Face parkas from ski team. A few of them talk to Robin, Bianca, and me. They ask for our phone numbers and a few days later, while we're watching *Days* at Robin's house, the phone rings. It's Ryan Combs, and even though I told her not to say anything, Robin tells him I think Duffy is cute. I grab the phone and tell Ryan Robin likes him and Bianca likes Jeff Burton. Robin and Bianca squeal and I hang up. By the end of the week they ask us out, but going out with someone from another school is weird. You never see them. You talk on the phone once in a while but don't have much to say.

Cascade has a Valentine's Day dance and they invite the Pilot Butte kids. Robin, Bianca, Kim, and I get a ride from Kim's Mom. Kim's mom is pretty and thin with long blonde hair. She's the cool mom. She does things my mom never does like smoke cigarettes, take diet pills, and drink wine or cocktails with dinner. On the drive we smear on lip-gloss and brush our hair. I look out the window as we cross the river. I'm nervous to see Duffy. I can barely remember what he looks like. We whisper and giggle our answers the same question: will you kiss him? I wonder if Duffy will try to kiss me. I rub my palms together to make them stop sweating. If he tries to kiss me, will I kiss him back?

We pull up to Cascade. It's the newer school; clean, whitewashed, and fresh compared to Pilot Butte. As we walk across the dark-black asphalt, it's hard to believe a whole other world of kids exist here with a whole different set of variables and equations.

Red paper hearts dangle from the ceiling in the cafeteria and we spot the boys hanging out in a corner. They aren't dancing, so we pretend they aren't there as we dance to the fast songs and try not to get caught peeking at them. We're waiting for a slow song and finally they play Phil Collins' "One More Night." The boys walk over. Ryan asks Robin, Jeff asks Bianca, and finally Duffy asks me, "You wanna dance?"

I take his hand and follow him to the middle of the Cascade cafeteria. I wrap my arms around his warm shoulders like I've seen older girls do. I feel the weight of his hands clasped around my waist, and I'm suddenly hot. He pulls me close, and I hope he can't feel my heart slamming against my chest. We shift our weight from one foot to the other as we turn in a tight circle. I rest my cheek on his shoulder and breathe in the smell of laundry detergent in his soft white t-shirt. My face feels hot, and I'm glad it's dark in the gym so he can't see me blushing. The song ends, and the lights in the gym come on. I pull away, scared that he might try to kiss me.

"See ya," I tell Duffy Bryant as I turn away. I can't look him in the eye.

"Yeah, see ya," he says back and that's it.

I'm upstairs listening to Q94, hoping they'll play "One More Night" when the phone rings. It's Ryan Combs. He tells me Duffy wants to break up. "He thinks you're cool and everything, but you guys never see each other."

He's right and at least he isn't breaking up because he thinks I'm lame. I calculate the failure of this relationship and wonder how much I will suffer because *he* broke up with *me*. "Okay," I say and I hang up the phone. I jump onto my bed and scream into my pillow. I will not cry. I walk back out to the hallway and dial Jamie's number. I stretch the cord into my room and tell her what happened.

"Whatever," she tells me. She never even met Duffy. "He seemed kind of lame."

"Yeah," I say. "That's what I thought."

If I act like I don't care, it doesn't hurt as much.

That night, I lay awake in the darkness. A car passes by, and I trace the headlights across the ceiling. The house sleeps around me, Chet and Mitch in their room, Laura in her room, Mom and Dad downstairs. I need to get Duffy out of my mind. The feeling of his arms draped across my shoulders and the smell of his cotton t-shirt gets added to the things I try not to think about as I fall asleep. What sneaks into my mind though, just before I drift off to sleep, is the worry that this could mean I'm not cool anymore. The worry doesn't keep me awake, but it lingers around the corners of my mind and seeps into my dreams.

Birds and Bees

It finally feels like spring in Bend when a string of days reach into the 50s. Jamie and I sprawl out on her waterbed listening to Q94. We study *Teen* and *Seventeen* magazines, glance at pictures and read articles about clothes, make-up, and enhancing our best features. We pour over sex and advice columns to tease out the meanings of words we overhear in the hallways: boner, masturbate, cum. We practice kissing on the backs of our hands. Jamie asks about my siblings, but even with two older brothers and an older sister there is so much I don't know about bodies, hormones, and growing up. Mom and Dad never talk about adolescence, where babies come from, or periods, so all I know is what I've seen in my older siblings. Chet and Mitch's voices crack and change. Laura goes bra shopping at JC Penny. I hear about moms having "the talk" with their kids and wonder what I'll learn when Mom sits me down for that conversation.

When I get home from Jamie's, I head upstairs to my room and find a book on my dresser. Mom works part time at First Chapter Books in the Wagner Mall. She must have thought of me when she saw *What's Happening to My Body: For Girls*. A girl and her mom smile on the purple cover. I flip to the table of contents and read headings for puberty, breasts, sex, and boys' bodies. I can't believe Mom left this book for me. I skim through the first few pages with line drawings of the male and female body parts. There are words, the *real* words, for the parts we never talk about. I close the bedroom door and lay across my bed. My heart pounds as I read. There is more information in this book than I ever wanted to know and it isn't just about girls. There are chapters about erections, ejaculations, and wet dreams. I can't decide who has it worse, boys or girls. Girls have periods with blood and cramps, which sounds pretty awful, but boy stuff seems even worse. They can't control their penises and get boners in the middle of class.

I read until it gets so dark in my room my eyes hurt. After the section about breasts I close the book and look around my room for a place to keep it where no one will find it. I shove it underneath my *Teen* and *Seventeen* magazines in the bottom drawer of my nightstand and head downstairs.

Mom watches TV on the living room couch. I sink into the lime green recliner.

"Did you see the book I left you?" Mom asks.

"Uh huh," I answer but I can't look at her.

"Do you have any questions?"

"Nope," I say as I tilt the chair all the way back. Mom turns back to the TV. She's watching *Cheers*. Sam and Diane flirt and tell jokes that I don't get. Mom falls asleep, and I wonder if that's it for my birds and bees talk.

Sex is another topic that gets buried in our family. I'm sure my friends' moms will have real heart-to-heart chats with them, but that's not how things work in the house on Jones Road.

I head back upstairs, walk past Laura's room, and wonder if Mom had "the talk" with her. I close my bedroom door and pull the book back out of the drawer. Maybe I'm lucky. Reading a book is a lot less awkward than a sex talk. I have a resource, an encyclopedia to find all the answers I need. I flip through the pages and absorb it all.

Turning 12

One night in April, Mom makes popcorn at the stove as I load the dishwasher. "So, who do you want to invite to your birthday party this year?" she asks as she shakes the pan of oil and kernels.

I think about who came to my birthday party last year, all the girls from St. Francis and Lori Bohnenkamp whose older sister plays basketball with Laura. This year I have a whole new group of friends. I start making the list in my head: Jamie, Michelle, Robin, Bianca, Kim, Stephanie Troutman, and Tracy Burnside. "How many can I invite?" I ask because I've never had a birthday without Loretta, and maybe if I invite Faith too, things will be better between us.

"How many are you thinking?"

I count but run out of fingers. "Um, like ten," I say.

The popcorn explodes in the pan like firecrackers. "Okay, make a list and we'll see who can make it."

Bianca and Loretta can't be there, but on a Saturday afternoon girls from different parts of my life come together. I introduce old friends to new ones and cross my fingers that everyone will get along. We play charades, open presents, eat Cherry Crunch and then head up to the family room. My new and old friends play ping-pong and video games on our old Atari as I sit on the couch with Jamie. Everything has gone just fine. Faith gets along with my new friends, and Lori makes everyone laugh, but as Jamie and I watch Tracy and Kim play video games, I wish everyone would leave. It's too much work making sure everyone gets along. I'm relieved when Mom yells upstairs that parents are here. My friends leave one at a time until I'm alone again. I start to think about next year's birthday party. I'm not sure what I'll want to do, but I know I want it to be totally different.

Best Friends

Jamie calls to tell me Michelle Meteer is moving. I'm sad she's leaving, but I'm also a little bit glad. Once Michelle is gone, I know Jamie and I will be even closer. I've already started hanging out at Jamie's more than Michelle does anyway. Besides, sometimes Michelle isn't that cool. She laughs too loud and wears fake Keds instead of real ones.

Jamie and I plan a going away party for Michelle at Pat and Mike's downtown with a balloon arch and a deejay. We invite tons of people and after we dance, drink punch, and eat cake we promise Michelle we'll write letters; keep in touch. Then she's gone and there's an empty desk in Mrs. Gregory's classroom.

The next weekend I stay the night over at Jamie's house. We're hanging out in her room, leaning against the solid wood of Jamie's waterbed.

"I know best friends are totally elementary school, but you're pretty much my best friend now," Jamie says as she brushes her hair upside down.

"Yeah," I tell her, "you're mine too."

We both look at one another. "Sweet!" We say in unison and laugh.

Jamie and I have sleepovers every weekend and call one another every night. We write notes in class and talk about Jamie's crush on Dally Taylor and how I still like Duffy. When I get in a fight with my mom, I call Jamie to tell her what happened. When Jamie gets a weird note from Kim, she shows me and we interpret it together. We share and hold one another's secrets. It's safe. Jamie and I solve the equations of middle school together. We never use the term best friends, but that's what we are. Jamie and I are inseparable.

Outdoor School

I'm the first in my family to be at Pilot Butte for sixth grade so I'm the only one to go to Outdoor School. Jamie (who has never spent more than a night away from home) is going too.

When we get off the bus at camp they divide us into groups and Jamie and I are separated. Without the comfort of my friends around me, I'm nervous, but counselors from the high school nicknamed Bear, Shroom, and Sage start us on an activity, so I forget my friends aren't around.

First, we do a solo hike. We walk off by ourselves and find a tree. I stand in the cool shade of a ponderosa pine and listen to people's footsteps as the other sixth graders disappear into the forest. I look up into the branches of my tree because that's what they told us to do. The wind blows through the needles and birds call to one another. I listen to my heartbeat and focus on each breath. It's been a long time since I've been alone, not thinking about anyone else, just being by myself. So much has changed this year. I used to worry about Mom and Dad getting a divorce, Chet going crazy from voices in his head, and fights with Laura and Mitch. But this year I've been concentrating on school and popularity. I've barely thought about my family at all. I almost start to cry, but before I can figure out why a whistle blows. A voice calls us in from the forest and I return to the world. I put on a smile to help me forget the thoughts that come with quiet.

We make nametags out of wood circles. We hike through old growth and use microscopes to look at pond water. We learn about the hydrogen cycle, and I hate the idea of dying and my body being eaten by bacteria and decomposing while the trees grow around me.

During a break on the last day, I head to the bathroom. I hold my breath in the stink and look down at something rusty and brown coating my underwear. I think it might have had some kind of accident and try to wipe it clean but can't. Luckily it doesn't smell. I vow not to tell anyone about this accident.

I don't realize I've started my period until I get home and the rusty brown turns red. I remember reading that I shouldn't freak out. I'm not dying. I'm becoming a woman.

I go downstairs to ask Mom for a maxi pad. She gives me a hug, and I roll my eyes. She leads me into the downstairs bathroom and shows me where she keeps the pads and tampons. I take a pad out of the box and Mom stares at our reflections the mirror.

"Can I tell your dad?" she asks.

I blush and shrug. "I don't care."

Mom puts her arm around me and kisses my forehead. "My baby is all grown up."

I stare at my bare feet on the bathroom rug. Mom leaves and I peel the backing off the pad and stick it to my underwear. When I pull my jeans up it feels like I'm wearing a diaper. I know this means I'm becoming a woman and everything, but I can't believe I'm going to have my period once a month for the rest of my life.

I head upstairs and close my bedroom door behind me. I pull my secret puberty book out of the drawer and reread the chapter on menstruation. I think about calling Jamie, but she hasn't started her period yet. Neither has Bianca, Robin, or Kim. I won't tell them. Even though that book has a whole chapter about it, starting your period isn't a big deal. I wonder if Mom is telling Dad, and suddenly I'm embarrassed. I don't want to talk about this, not to Mom or Laura or Jamie. I pretend my period isn't happening. I bury it like Chet's anti-depressants and Mom and Dad's therapy sessions. My period becomes another secret.

Chet's Graduation

The gym at Mountain View High School is packed for graduation. The basketball court is covered with folding chairs and a stage. Laura sits on the risers with the choir while Mom, Dad, Mitch, and I wait in the stands. The band plays *Pomp and Circumstance* as the graduates file in. Mom and Dad look at one another and smile. Dad holds Mom's hand and I can't remember the last time they've done that. The melody of the march gets stuck in my head as I crane my neck to catch a glimpse of Chet in his graduation robe and gold honors cord. I spot him, handsome and tan from baseball. He looks happy. Mom and Dad cheer just like they did at Chet's football, basketball, and baseball games.

Mom and Dad have been praying for Chet at mass every Sunday, and I guess you could say God answered them. Chet did great on the SAT and is going to the University of Oregon next fall. He went to prom with a beautiful blonde in a strapless pale pink dress. Chet has had the perfect senior year.

After speeches and songs they finally call Chet's name. He steps across the stage and I stand and cheer with the rest of the family. After the ceremony, we look for Chet in the crowd. He hugs friends, teammates, and teachers, and when he sees us he hugs us too.

I'm glad everything has worked out for Chet, but I doubt God had anything to do with it. I don't go to Catholic school, or Confession anymore. Sunday mass is boring and I hardly think about God. I pray for Duffy to call me but he hasn't. Maybe if I'd stayed at St. Francis or if God talked to me when I prayed, I'd feel differently, but I didn't stay at St. Francis, and when I pray all I hear is silence. Chet's fine, but I don't think God had anything to do with it.

Summer

It's cool to stay busy on vacation so I baby-sit for a few families from church, take care of our neighbors' pets, and join the swim team with Robin. Jamie goes to Los Angeles to visit her aunt and grandmother. Kim goes to the coast and Bianca leaves for horse camp.

In July our family drives to San Diego. We stay with Aunt Bev and our cousins in a condo at the beach. We make sandwiches, drink ice-cold Cokes, and lay out at the beach with our blonde cousins. At night we stay up late and watch John Hughes movies.

For the rest of July, I hang out with Jamie. We lie on her waterbed, listen to music, and read magazines. The afternoon sun floods Jamie's room heating it up like a sauna, so we walk over to 7-11 for Slurpees, and when we come back we watch *Days* in the living room. On super hot days we hang out at the mall, plan our back-to-school shopping, or go to the movies. We watch *Top Gun* three times.

In August, Mitch has his birthday party up at Scout Lake. He invites Shawn Maniscalco, a boy who will be in eighth grade with Mitch. He has blonde hair and a hot tan. I ride in the front seat next to Mom while Mitch, Shawn, and another friend ride in the backseat. It's a perfect day at the lake: hot and sunny. I'm comfortable in the turquoise swim team suit I wore in California, but I wish I had a bikini like my cousin, Traci. I'm sure I'd look more mature. We swim, eat lunch, and when Mitch blows out the candles on his cake, I make a wish too. I dream I'm Shawn's girlfriend and that the two of us could spend the summer at the lake together. Then, when school starts again we'd be going out and everyone would wonder what happened between Nori and Shawn over the summer.

After Mitch's birthday, I can't stop thinking about Shawn. I ask Mitch to invite him over but Mitch didn't have as much fun on his birthday as I did. I practice writing Nori Maniscalco in cursive. I study Shawn's picture in the yearbook and decide he is by far the cutest eighth grader. I forget all about Niko Gonzales and Duffy Bryant. Now, all I think about is Shawn Maniscalco.

For Jamie's birthday her mom takes us to see *Stand By Me* even though it's rated R. We've been waiting for this movie all summer because it was filmed in Oregon and River Phoenix is in it. It's a story about boys set in the 50s, but it's really about us. We leave the theatre with Ben E. King's song in our heads and a whole new vocabulary. We give one another skins and two for flinching. Instead of saying bye it's, "See you later," followed by, "Not unless I see you first." Mom buys me the soundtrack since it has so many songs she remembers from when she was a teenager. Jamie and I try to figure out who is who from the movie. Everyone wants to be Chris (he's the coolest) but I'm more like Gordy because I love to write, so that makes Jamie is Chris. Bianca and Robin are like Vern and Teddy. They're both funny and a little bit crazy.

Labor Day Weekend comes, but there isn't an adventure to find a dead body, a pie-eating contest, or river full of leeches. Instead, the carnival comes to town. The middle school kids hang out around the towering metal rides: The Zipper and Tilt-a-Wheel. Bianca, Robin, and I wait in line for the Zipper with two eighth grade girls, Caren and Melanie. Melanie asks Caren if Shawn's coming and the mere mention of his name makes my heart beat fast. Bianca and I exchange a look. We both think Shawn is cute and I'm sure Bink is just as excited as I am by the possibility that he could be here tonight.

"No, he's out of town," Caren says as Bianca, Robin, and I pile into the cage of The Zipper. I wonder if Caren is going out with Shawn. Even though Shawn and I went to the lake together for Mitch's birthday, that's the only time we've ever spent together. I've been obsessing over him, imagining what he's been doing all summer, picturing us together, but he probably hasn't thought about me once. The ride lurches forward, and I can't believe I've wasted so much time thinking about this boy who hardly knows me. Robin and Bianca lean forward and our cage tilts.

"Come on, Nor," Bianca yells. "Lean."

I shift my weight forward and our cage starts to spin. I promise myself I'll never get hung up on a boy like that again. We lean together and the cage rotates faster and faster. We scream and spin around and around and around until I don't know up from down. Robin, Bianca, and I tumble off the ride, arm in arm, leaning on one another for support; thrilled by the power of our own momentum.

The carnival ride makes me forget about Shawn. As long as I have my friends with me, as long as we're all moving in the same direction, we'll be just fine.

Family Therapy

It's been a year since Chet's hospitalization. Before he leaves for college, his counselor wants the family to come in for a session. Mom, Dad, and Chet ride in the station wagon while Laura drives Mitch and me in the Datsun. I haven't told anyone, not even Jamie, that my family is going to see a shrink. If someone sees us walk into the doctor's office, the whole town will think we're crazy.

The inside of the doctor's office looks different than I expected. There's a couch, like I thought there would be, but the room is bright; so full of light. I'd imagined a dark, wood-paneled room. There is a big green plant in the corner, and while we wait for the counselor I study it and wonder if it's real. The leaves are so bright and perfect. I want to get up and feel it, but I'm too nervous. I want to know if a real plant could grow in the middle of this psychiatrist's office.

Our family barely fits in all of the chairs in the room, and we sit in age order: Chet, Laura, Mitch, and then me scrunched together on the couch. Mom sits in a chair on one side of the couch, and Dad sits next to her.

The psychiatrist comes in and talks to Chet first. He makes steady eye contact as if Chet's the only one in the crowded room. I doubt this guy has ever had so many people in his office at one time. While he talks with Chet I try to imagine everything this man must know about my brother. I know Chet sat there and didn't talk the first few sessions like in the movie *Ordinary People* where the kid's brother died and it was the other brother's fault and his parents were awful about the whole thing. I can't imagine Chet being like that, hating himself and wanting to die, but maybe he is. Maybe this guy knows what's really going on and I don't know my brother at all.

The counselor introduces himself and he already knows our names. "You must be Laura, Mitch, and Nori," he says as he looks at each of us and shakes our hands. His palm is warm and soft. After shaking his hand, I sink back into the couch and wait.

"So, I want to thank you all for coming in today. Chet and I have been meeting for about a year now, and Mom and Dad," he nods at my parents. "You've been in for a couple of sessions, and well, we thought it would be a good idea to have the whole family here before Chet heads off to college."

I look over at Mom. She has a worried look on her face. She's about to cry.

"So Chet, do you want to explain why we're here."

Chet starts talking. "Well, last year, after Bethy Hurley died, you know, Mom and Dad put me in the hospital to help me sleep and settle down." He takes a deep breath. He sounds so different, so grown up. "They took me to the hospital even though I didn't want to go, and they were doing what they thought was best for me." Chet takes another deep breath and I can tell he's practiced the words tumbling out of his mouth. "So, I'm doing a lot better now and I just want you guys to know that I'm okay and if any thing like this happens to you, make sure you let Mom and Dad know so they can help."

I hear everything Chet says and study the plant in the corner of the room. I feel myself breathing, letting out some air I didn't even know I was holding in my lungs. Chet isn't saying anything new, but he's never talked about it before. None of us have talked about the days leading up to Chet going into the hospital or how angry he was when he came back. We never talk about what happened while he was gone or how he didn't smile for what seems like forever. No one says anything about how Mom and Dad were so worried about Chet that Laura, Mitch, and I disappeared.

The counselor asks Laura how she felt when Chet was in the hospital. I think back to last summer, which seems longer than a year ago. I remember Chet coming home from Young Life camp talking too fast with eyes too wide open. I knew there was something wrong and tried to figure it out but there were way too many unknown variables. Laura says she was scared, that she didn't understand what was happening and her words match my thoughts.

"And Mitch," the counselor turns to Mitch. He asks him about his adoption and how he feels about Chet and what happened. Mitch says pretty much the same thing Laura did.

When it's my turn I don't really know how I feel. I don't think I feel any differently than Laura and Mitch, so I stick with the script. "It was scary, confusing." I don't mention how I spied on Chet to try to find out why he was blaring U2 in his bedroom when he first started hearing the voices. I don't say how alone I felt when the rest of us were left to cope with life on our own. I don't mention Laura's stress fracture or how Mitch and I started at a new school but none of that seemed significant compared to what Chet was going through.

Mom and Dad want us to know how terrible they feel about what happened. Mom says if we ever can't sleep or ever hear voices, we have to tell them.

I look back at the plant in the corner and all of the words coming out of our mouths seem artificial. I imagine myself, years in the future, sitting in this room because I've been hospitalized, because I couldn't sleep and started hearing voices. I study the bright green leaves on the plant and a tiny fear grows in the corner of my mind. If it happened to Chet, it could happen to Laura, or Mitch, or me. I don't know the rules for insanity. It might be like a math problem where you use the distributive property. If Chet is crazy maybe we all are and Laura, Mitch, and I will eventually go nuts. Or maybe, it's genetic instead of contagious so Mitch's adoption will protect him from going mad.

The doctor asks if we have any questions or anything else to say. I feel a window closing on this conversation. Our family hasn't talked about this since last summer even though it colored every moment of the year. This could be the last time we talk about it for a very long time. If I don't say something now this will get buried just like all the other problems we never talk about: internment camp, Uncle George's suicide, how different we are from Mom's family and everyone in Bend. I try to think of something to say, but instead of asking if crazy is contagious, or if something like this could happen to me I ask, "Is that plant over there real?" and as soon as the words leak out, I realize how crazy I sound.

The End and Beginning

On the last day of summer Mom and Dad plan what Chet needs for college. Laura has a boot on her foot and hopes that in a few months the stress fracture in her foot will heal for basketball season. School starts tomorrow and although Mitch and I will both be at Pilot Butte, we'll do what we usually do: ignore one another.

I shut my bedroom door to everything going on in the house on Jones Road: Chet packing, Laura clomping up and down the stairs; Mitch brewing a quiet hatred of me. I slide the *Stand By Me* tape in my boom box and Buddy Holly sings, "Everyday it's a gettin' closer, goin' faster than a roller coaster, love like yours will surely come my way."

Earlier, at Jamie's house, we decided on our outfits for the first day. We have to look accidentally perfect; like we stumbled upon these clothes and don't care all that much about what we wear on the first day of school.

"Everyday seems a little longer, every way loves a little stronger, come what may, do you ever long for true love from me?"

I hum as I lay clothes out on my dresser and pack the canvas bag I'll be using this school year. My new notebook is stocked with notebook paper, dividers, new pens, and pencils. I slide into bed but can't fall asleep. I push the window open and look into the clear, cool night. The light in Robin's bedroom across the street glows in the darkness. I wonder what she's wearing for the first day. We haven't talked about it, but I know in the morning Robin and I will meet on Jones Road. We will turn our backs on our families and walk to school. We'll check out one another's outfits and hair. I'll make sure Robin looks okay and she'll make sure I do too. We'll discuss new schedules and possibilities for the school year. Seventh grade will start just like sixth grade ended: Robin and I walking to and from school together.

Seventh Grade

Intro to Social Studies

On the first day of seventh grade I wear old faded Levi's because even with all of the money I saved up babysitting, mowing lawns, and helping Mitch with his paper route, I still can't afford Guess Jeans. But the Swatch Rugby, Levis, and Stan Smiths make the coolest outfit I've ever had. I'm tan from the summer, my hair is cut in a bob, and I feel confident.

I walk to school with Robin and we stop to pick up Bianca just like last year. When we get to school we find Kim and Jamie in C hall. As cool as I might look, Jamie looks even better. She's had one of those over-the-summer-makeovers like in the movies. She got her braces off and her hair is bright blonde from the summer sun. The biggest change, though, is that instead of thick glasses, now she wears contacts.

We hang out until the bell rings and then scatter to class. No one is in my homeroom, so I head down to D Hall by myself. I choose a seat by the door and Walker Stewart, Stephanie Troutman, and Melanie Jacobson come in. Then I see Loretta. I could ignore her just like she ignored me on the first day last year, but so much has happened since then that I don't really care. Besides, this isn't St. Francis. Pilot Butte is completely different. Loretta smiles at me, and I smile back. She sits a couple seats away, and her hands shake as she fidgets with her backpack. We wait for Ms. Lacrouix to finish roll, and I pretend not to see how uncomfortable my old friend looks. Ms. Lacrouix tells us to choose locker partners. Stephanie and Melanie pair up. I look down hoping to be the last one left so I won't have to share with anyone, but Loretta leans toward me.

"Wanna be partners?"

I pause. Loretta is wearing the right things and her blonde spiral curls are cute. None of my friends are here to share with so I say, "Sure," with a shrug and act like being Loretta's locker partner is no big deal.

After homeroom I go to the wood shop; a huge room filled with tools and machines. I breathe in the smell of sawdust as Mr. Jones describes the wooden ducks, grocery list holders, and coasters we'll make.

At break I head back to C Hall and find Bianca and Robin at their locker struggling with the combination.

"My locker's in D Hall," I scowl.

"Bummer," Robin says as she twists the lock. Gabe and Ezra's locker is at the end of the hall, and I see Cody French, a boy from St. Francis, talking to them. Jason Davis is there too and Bianca smiles at him. Robin still can't get the locker open (probably because she keeps looking at Gabe). She shows me the combo and I twist the lock to clear it.

"Gabe is so hot," Robin says as I twirl the series of numbers. It's Robin's turn to like Gabe. It's only a matter of time before she asks me to talk to him for her. I've never liked Gabe, so I'm stuck being the messenger. I open Bianca and Robin's locker and head to class.

After lunch I walk into the choir room and finally see Shawn Maniscalco. He's in the front with the other boys whose voices have changed like Bruce Mitchell and Mark Roberts. I sit in the back with Bink and the rest of the altos, but it's perfect because I can watch Shawn the whole time. I haven't seen him since Mitch's birthday, and I can hardly believe he's right there, so tan and blonde. He is definitely the hottest eighth grader. I try to work up the nerve to say hi to him, to figure out what might make me stand out among all the other girls at Pilot Butte. How can I help him remember that we went to the lake together this summer; that I'm the girl of his dreams?

After choir it's social studies with Mrs. McAdams. She tells us we'll study ancient civilizations, class hierarchies, and social structures. I flip through the pages of the thick textbook; scan pictures of pyramids and ancient ruins. I wish someone had studied Pilot Butte this way. If there was a chapter about sixth, seventh, and eighth grade at Pilot Butte I could just read about how things work instead of spending so much time and energy trying to figure out how to be cool; how to get and stay popular. I guess that's all seventh grade is: a long lesson in social studies.

Volleyball Set Up

After school I rush out of the girls' locker room with the other seventh and eighth grade girls for volleyball practice. The florescent light in the gym makes everyone's skin look green and the dingy kneepads seem even dirtier.

We line up to stretch but keep an eye on the door to see the boys peek into the gym before they head out to football practice. After stretches Miss Wilson and Mrs. Holt show us how to pass the ball back and forth, hands locked, forearms butterflied flat. We form two long lines across the gym and try to line up across from our friends. Jamie and I manage to be across from one another and we practice passing. The ball stings each time it hits my arms and even though I try to get the ball to bounce right to Jamie we can hardly pass it back and forth twice before the ball sails over my head or bounces across the gym. It doesn't really matter though because volleyballs explode all over the gym like popcorn popping in a pan.

Miss Wilson blows her whistle and tells us to rotate so we all have new partners. Jamie heads to the left and partners up with Robin. Kim is my partner now and we do a little better, passing the ball back and forth three or four times.

Miss Wilson blows the whistle again and now I'm stuck with Valerie Segerstrom. She has the reddest cheeks I've ever seen and black hair she's trying to grow out. Bianca, Jamie, and I make fun of Val's split ends and even though she sits right next to us in English, we ignore her. Valerie wants to be friends but for some reason we don't want to be friends with her. She just isn't cool. She hasn't figured out that you can't act like you care. Bianca sees Val and I are partners and gives me a smirk. I roll my eyes and throw the ball toward Valerie. She passes it right back to me, nice and high so I can move my feet and pass it back to her. We pass it back and forth the whole time until Miss Wilson blows the whistle. I want to smile because it was fun passing the ball so well, but Val and I aren't friends so I don't smile at all.

The smooth flesh of my forearms is bright pink and I rub my palms across the hot skin while Ms. Wilson demonstrates the overhand set. Laura used to set for the varsity team at Mountain View before her stress fracture, so I've practiced this with her. Ms. Wilson has us set with our partners, and I can tell on her first touch Valerie has done this before too. The ball soars between us and I only have to take a tiny step or two before sending the ball back through the air. Ms. Wilson blows the whistle and I think we're going to switch partners again, but instead she asks Val and me to come to the front of the gym. My face is hot and my arms burn. I can't believe I'm stuck in the front of everyone with her. This could ruin me.

We set the ball back and forth as Ms. Wilson repeats instructions to the other girls, "See how their hands are soft and they bend their legs with each set."

I hope I look as miserable as I feel so no one thinks I like Valerie. I move my feet beneath my fifth set and as the ball falls toward me my fingers suddenly stiffen up and the muscles in my arms contract at the wrong time. The ball smacks right off my forehead.

I fall to the floor as if I took a bullet to the head. My eyes water, and I think I might cry, but then I hear laughter. I join them because that must have looked hilarious. Bianca, Robin, Kim, and Jamie laugh along with everyone else, but Miss Wilson looks annoyed. She sends Valerie and me back into line and tells us to rotate partners again even though everyone's still laughing. My partner is Robin now and we struggle to set and pass, but I don't care. Val is someone else's partner and hopefully no one will remember that I was playing with her the day the volleyball hit me in the head. It was a close call, but I managed to balance fitting in and standing out.

Friday Night Football

On Friday afternoon we pass notes in Mrs. McAdams' class to find out what's going on tonight. By the end of the period it's decided: everyone's going to the Mountain View football game. Last year I watched every game with Mom, Dad, and Mitch while Laura played in the band. We kept a careful eye on number 24 but Chet has graduated and is about to leave for college. Mom and Dad have no reason to go to games, so Mitch and I ride with Laura to the high school. Instead of watching the game, I hang out by the concession stand with the other middle school kids.

The night is freezing cold. Everyone bundles up in parkas, scarves, and mittens but body warmth is what keeps you really warm. The eighth grade boys stand behind their girlfriends and pretend to watch the game. That's when I see Shawn and Caren. Shawn's wearing a red, white, and blue parka and Nikes. Caren has on a bright white jacket and pink gloves. They're cute and I'm jealous, but Caren is nice and Shawn looks really happy. I try not to stare at them keeping one another warm.

Robin and Gabe are going out and even though most of the seventh graders haven't figured out the whole going out thing, by half time, Bianca is going out with Peter Moore. The couples sneak up off to the baseball field during the third quarter. I try to watch the game but I don't really see what's happening. I imagine what's going on at the baseball field. I know from social studies that a boy heading to the cold dark of the baseball field elevates his social status while a girl risks getting a bad reputation. Maybe that's I'm so annoyed with Robin and Bianca. Or maybe I wish someone wanted to keep me warm in the cold dark of the baseball field.

Laura drives Mitch and me home after the game and reminds us that we should be able to tell Mom and Dad the score. I look at her blankly. "We lost, 21-7, Nori." She's annoyed with me. "Did you watch any of the game?"

"Yeah," I lie.

"She was hanging out with her little friends by the concession stand," Mitch adds.

"Shut up, Mitch," I sneer and stare out the window into the darkness. I wish it was last year when going to games was easy. I sat with Mom, Dad, and Mitch. I watched Chet and didn't worry about hanging out with the right people. It didn't matter who I liked, or who might like me. Last year I didn't have to wonder what my friends were doing in the cold dark of the baseball field on a Friday night.

Expanding Horizons

Laura, Mitch, and I stand next to the garage as Chet packs the last of his stuff into the car. Mom tells Laura dinner is in the fridge and then joins Dad in the car. We hug Chet goodbye. He waves from the driver's seat and then backs the station wagon up the steep driveway. We wave as he drives away, and I try to smile even though I feel like crying.

I head inside and turn on the baseball game. That's what we would have done with Chet still here. I watch the batter warm up and think of the 100 swings Chet used to take every night here in the living room. Now he's gone. It's quiet without Chet talking through the game, and I realize just how much space my oldest brother occupied in the house on Jones Road.

Without him around, I wonder what will tether our house to the ground. Mom and Dad are still concerned about how he will do at school, but Mom's always worried about something: money, how much sugar we eat, the Reagan Administration, or death squads in Central America, but since Chet's hospitalization her worry has been connected to him. Maybe out of habit, even from 100 miles away, Chet will continue to hold us together.

Between innings I think about how things will never be the same. Laura is the oldest now and our family will only be together when Chet comes home for vacations. I imagine Chet, Mom, and Dad driving away from us and wish I could go away to college. I would party with my friends, drink beer, order pizza, and live in a dorm with no parents around. I could do whatever I want. It sounds perfect. But I don't get to see Chet's new dorm or the cafeteria where he'll eat. I'm stuck here in the house on Jones Road eating meals from Mom's kitchen.

Jamie calls, so I turn off the game and I head up to my room where thoughts of Chet and college fade away with the evening light.

Chet calls on Sunday nights. After he talks to Mom sometimes I get on the phone and we talk about sports or music. Last year Chet got me *The Dream of the Blue Turtles* (even though he was bummed The Police broke up). I studied the liner notes until I understood "Russians" and "We Work the Black Seam." Chet asks if I've listened to U2's Unforgettable Fire or the old Police albums. I haven't, so the next time I'm at the record store at the mall, instead of looking at Whitney Houston and Phil Collins, I browse through albums Chet has told me about: Dire Straights, Talking Heads, and Midnight Oil. I pick through used records and cracked tape cases, and my world expands beyond Bend, Oregon. Instead of '80s pop music about sex, parties, and money, music becomes political and academic: aborigines in Australia, nuclear warheads in Russia, apartheid in South Africa. Chet has only moved a hundred miles away, but on Sunday nights his phone calls carry me away from small-town life. I can see beyond Bend, and my world grows exponentially.

Birthday Party Invitations

Mrs. McAdams teaches us about serfs and peasants, tradesmen and artisans, priests and royalty. This social structure isn't so different from what plays out at Pilot Butte. The cool eighth graders sit at the top of the pyramid: pretty and perfect. They have money, nice houses, and cool clothes. Then there are the popular seventh graders: Robin, Bianca, Kim, Jamie, me, and our other friends: Stephanie Troutman, Melissa Jacobson, and Roxanne Langhaim. There are cool sixth graders, but we haven't figured out who they are and since we're seventh graders we don't really care.

Jamie and I have made it. We're cool, but on Thursday in Mrs. McAdam's class, when I ask Kim if she wants to go with us to see *Ferris Bueller's Day Off* on Friday night she says she can't. She's busy. Robin and Bianca tell me the same thing on the walk home and after a few tense steps Robin tells me, "We're going to Kim's birthday party."

I try not to look hurt as we pause at Bianca's driveway.

"I'm sure her mom only let her invite a certain number of people," Bianca adds.

"It's okay," I say but I'm hurt. Kim came to my birthday last spring so I think she should have invited me. "I'm sure you guys will have fun."

Jamie and I show up to see *Ferris Bueller* at the Mountain View Mall on Friday night and a bunch of eighth graders are there. We say hi to Caren and Melanie, Shawn and Kevin. Last year I figured out that if cool eighth graders like you, it helps your popularity. I suddenly don't care that we aren't at Kim's birthday party. It's way better to be hanging out at the movies with all the eighth graders.

I love the movie even though I've never skipped school or faked being sick to stay home. Ferris Bueller is the coolest especially when he sings "Twist and Shout" in the middle of a parade. He makes me want to go to a city where I can go to museums and stare at art, or to the ballpark and yell, "Hey batter, batter, batter, swing batter."

After the movie Jamie and I hang out at the mall and look at clothes at the Emporium. We make note of who was there because on Monday morning we can say that we saw *Ferris Bueller* and everyone was there.

On the walk to school on Monday Bianca asks me about my weekend and I don't even feel bad saying, "It was awesome. Jamie and I went to see *Ferris Bueller's Day Off* and everyone was there. We hung out the mall and saw tons of people. Tons." I ask about Kim's birthday but don't really care about the answer.

Social Studies Quiz

Jamie, Bianca, Kim, and I finish our lunches and leave the cafeteria shocked that Robin sat with the eighth graders again.

"Can you believe her?"

Robin broke up with Gabe last week and started going out with an eighth grade boy. She stopped hanging out with us and started hanging out with all the eighth graders.

"She thinks she's so cool."

We head down the hill toward the field. The cool eighth grade girls follow behind us. They stop and lean against the back of the gym. They're laughing about something and Robin laughs with them.

"She's so lame."

"Totally."

It's like we're in the cage of The Zipper, the carnival ride we rode before school started. That summer night Robin, Bianca, and I leaned and sent the cart spinning. Today Robin is on the outside and Jamie, Bianca, Kim, and I lean without her. We walk across the field and avoid eye contact with Robin, but I doubt she notices. She might be in with the eighth graders, but she doesn't see she's out with us.

For a few afternoons, the walk home from school is quiet. Bianca and I don't say anything to Robin and she doesn't say anything to us. All I hear is our feet padding along the asphalt of Shepard Road until Bianca finally says, "So, Robin, why aren't you hanging out with us anymore?"

"What do you mean?" Robin asks.

Bianca and I look at one another sideways. There's no way Robin doesn't know what we're talking about. I have to say something since Bianca brought it up.

"It's like you think you're better than us 'cause you're hanging out with the eighth graders now."

"It's not like that. I'm going out with J.T. and Sheri likes Gabe, so I've been talking to her. What do you expect me to do?"

I shrug my shoulders and Bianca heads into her house without another word.

Robin and I set off toward home. She walks fast like we're racing home, and I try to slow her down. "Robin, wait. Listen, we just don't want you to keep ditching us."

"I'm not ditching you guys," Robin says, exasperated. "You could come with me. You could hang out with them too."

I imagine hanging out with Robin and the other eighth graders, maybe even Shawn. The possibility excites me, but leaving Jamie, Bianca, and Kim would be terrible. I couldn't take the momentum of the three of them turning against me. "I couldn't," I say. "Having two totally different groups of friends would be hard. I mean, the eighth graders are nice but," I pause, unsure if I should say it. "I get it if you'd rather hang out with them."

Robin looks at me because she knows I'm really saying she has to choose: them or us.

We walk the length of Jones Road in silence and when I cross the street to my house I say, "See you in the morning?"

"Yep," Robin says and she walks away.

That night Bianca calls and we talk about what happened. "Well, we'll see what she does tomorrow," Bianca says.

The next day at lunch Robin sits with us at lunch. She and Bianca are back to being friends. Bianca lets up and the momentum of the four of us against Robin lifts. Robin is in again. She passes this social studies quiz and figures out how to be the coolest seventh grader. She still talks to the cool eighth grade girls, but she always comes back to us. Every time she goes we watch her. We act like it's no big deal. Robin climbs higher and higher on the social pyramid and in the complicated social structure of middle school, we watch for her to fall.

Mitch's Citizenship

When I was four my family adopted my brother Mitch from Korea. He arrived in a red jogging suit and green rubber shoes that smelled like Korea. He couldn't speak a single word of English, and I didn't think we would keep him because he cried and screamed and Dad had to carry him through the airport. He didn't want to go home with us, but Mom told me we couldn't return Mitch like something you buy from the store. He was staying for good.

At first it was hard. Mitch didn't like our food or the bunk beds in the room he shared with Chet. He had to learn how to ride a bike, play soccer, and go to church. But after a year or so, Mitch picked up English, and he became my biggest rival. In other families kids play with together, but in our family we play *against* one another. There's *always* a winner and a loser. Mitch and I race bikes in the field, play horse on the basketball court, and keep away with a soccer ball in the backyard. I can barely remember what our family was like before Mitch came. Mitch and I have always been competitive, but middle school makes things even worse. Mitch hates my friends. "I can't believe you hang out with those girls," he tells me with a scowl. He thinks Bianca is a snob and Kim is fake, but I don't care what Mitch thinks of my friends.

Mitch has a card from when he first came, when he was new to our family and our country. Along the top it says: RESIDENT ALIEN. When I first saw it I couldn't believe my brother was an alien like ET, but Mom says it's just a word they use for someone foreign. If the kids at school found out Mitch was an alien he'd get teased like crazy, and so would I, so I'm thankful when Mom and Dad decide it's time for Mitch to become a citizen.

Mitch studies U.S. History and memorizes our Senators and the preamble to the U.S. Constitution: "We the people of the United States of America, in order to form a more perfect

Union, establish Justice, insure domestic Tranquility..." But instead of taking an exam in Mr. Hess's U.S. History class, Mitch gets to miss school and drive with Mom and Dad to Salem for the citizenship test. He passes and recites the Pledge of Allegiance in a room with other new Americans. When they get home Mom has a family celebration planned. Mitch didn't tell anyone at school about this and Mom and Dad don't invite anyone over for the party, but Chet calls to offer his congratulations and Mom bakes a cake.

Mitch seems embarrassed by the whole ordeal. He doesn't like being reminded that, in a family that is already so different from everyone else in town (no other Asians or multiracial families), he is the different one, the adopted one; the Korean one. You can tell by looking, but we never talk about it.

Mitch isn't an alien anymore. He's officially American, but as we eat citizenship cake I can't help but remember how I felt when we were in LA for Grandma and Grandpa's anniversary. Even though we were with family, Mom's family looks nothing like us. They are all blonde and sun-kissed and we don't belong. Mom cleans up crumbs from the dining room table and I wonder if deep down Mitch feels like he's one of us, or if he still feels like an outsider.

Ice Skating

Just before Thanksgiving the first snow of winter falls, and the rink at the Inn of the Seventh Mountain opens. Jamie, Robin, Bianca, Kim, and I plan to go Friday night, and I'm pretty sure Mom will let me go. Anything can happen on a night up at the Inn, and I'd be devastated if I missed out. We invite everybody, but Gabe, Cougar, and Cody are hunting, so it's just us girls.

I'm surprised Mom agrees to drive us because there's a trace of snow on the ground, but she takes Robin, Jamie, and me slowly through town and up to The Inn. The little rink is lit up beneath a starry winter sky.

"Have fun," Mom says as we step out of the car and Jamie and Robin thank her for the ride. "I'll pick you up at nine. Don't be late."

"OK, Mom, bye," I say as I slam the door. I can't get away fast enough. I sprint to catch up with Jamie and Robin and hope Mom pulls away before anyone sees our old beat-up car. Our station wagon pulls away and I feel free. Three full hours without any adults around makes the night electric with possibility.

We rent skates, and the brown boots smell like dirty feet. The leather is stiff and cold, but I shove my feet in anyway, lace up, and wobble onto the ice. I've skated before, on the pond at Shevlyn Park, and Dad's words echo in my ears, "Keep your ankles stiff; lean into your turn just like skiing." Jamie hasn't been on skates much. She shuffles across the ice with one hand on the wooden wall. Robin has taken a few lessons. She crosses her feet in the turns and skates backward, peering over her shoulder like a professional. Robin is the coolest again. I'm somewhere between the two of them, skating around the rink, occasionally pounding into the wooden walls, laughing, and watching the parking lot for Bianca and Kim and anyone else who might show up to tonight.

The rink fills with little kids and their parents and then Bianca, Kim, and a few other girls from school: Stephanie Troutman, Amy Oliver, Loretta Garretson, and Tara Transue show up. We spot boys from Cascade, not Duffy, but Ryan Combs, Todd Hoffman, and Peter Moore as they fly around the rink on hockey skates.

When they clear the ice for the Zamboni everyone crowds around the counter to return rentals. My feet ache and the warm, ripe room makes me claustrophobic. I yank my feet from the skates and hurry outside.

Robin, Jamie, Bianca, Kim, and I walk to the café to get cocoa but Jamie and I only have a couple of quarters, so we hang out in the arcade. The boys from Cascade are there and after watching me beat Jamie at air hockey, Peter Moore and Todd Hoffman challenge us to a match. We slam the slippery disk back and forth and even though I score first, I think Jamie misses on purpose. The air shuts off and Peter and Todd win.

We head back out into the cold and walk along one of the wooded paths. Kim and Robin follow Peter, Todd, and Ryan to a clearing in the dark. The tree branches have kept any snow from falling here, and we kneel on a bed of springy pine needles. An empty Pepsi bottle sits in the middle of our circle, and I look over at Jamie, unsure how to handle this. There isn't anything in the book Mom gave me about how to handle a game of Spin the Bottle, but Jamie's whispering something to Kim so I shift on my heels and try to slow my racing heart. I look around the circle. I don't want my first real kiss to be like this. I pecked Jimmy Olson in fifth grade, and dream of kissing Duffy or Shawn, but I never thought of kissing Todd or Peter or Ryan.

Robin is bold, fearless, and she spins the bottle first. It lands on Kim. They giggle and Robin pecks Kim on the cheek. Peter goes next and the first time he spins it lands on Ryan. We laugh but Peter immediately spins again. There must be some kind of divot in the dirt because it lands on Kim again, and Peter kisses her on the lips. Everyone giggles and oohs.

It's my turn next. Thank God it's dark so no one can see how red my face is and my gloves conceal my sweaty palms.

"Come on, Nori, spin," Robin demands.

I spin the bottle fast. We watch as it turns through the dirt and then slows, slows, slows. It stops on Todd and I freeze not knowing what to do. Before I can even think Todd leans over, his warm face in mine, and kisses me quickly on the lips before pulling back to his spot.

"It's 9:00." Bianca says glancing at her Swatch. "We've got to go." Before there's the chance for any more spins, we sprint through the dark to the parking lot. We laugh about what just happened on the forest floor and measure tonight against every other night in our lives. This might have been the best night ever.

We reach the skating rink just as the headlights of the station wagon turn into the lot. We tumble into the warmth of the car, and the excitement of the night fizzles away. I'm glad we left the boys behind us so they won't see the family car. We climb in and Mom asks if we had a good time.

"Yeah," I answer as I peer over my shoulder to see Bianca, Robin, and Jamie smiling in the dark of the back seat.

"Oh, good," Mom says as she navigates the streets of Bend, completely unaware of the girl I am with my friends: the girl who skates fast and hangs out with the cool kids, the girl who plays air hockey because she doesn't have money for cocoa, the girl who plays Spin the Bottle with boys in the dark.

I grin at my friends sitting in the back seat, all of us trying to hold on to the magic of the night just a little bit longer.

Audition

In the winter of the seventh grade the local theatre company holds auditions for *The Best Christmas Pageant Ever*. I read the book in fifth grade and convince Jamie, Bianca, and Robin to try out. We stand in line at the theatre downtown and fill out forms with our names, ages, and any previous experience. I was in *The King and I* when I was five and played the Vice President in *Daniel, Darius and DeLion* at St. Francis, so I hope that will help me get a role, but there are way more kids than I expected. Robin, Bianca, Jamie, and I head inside and sit on the stage with the rest of the kids. Two women hand out scripts and call names. When my name is called I move to a mark on the stage, read my lines, and watch the two women make notes and say thank you. I try to figure out what they're looking for, but everyone's audition sounds the same to me. They say they'll call if we have a part, and we all leave hoping.

On the early morning walk to school Bianca says, "Did they call you last night?"

Robin and I shake our heads. I turn to Bianca, "You got a part, huh?" I'm annoyed. Bianca didn't even want to go to the audition. I practically forced her.

"I'm going to be Beth, you know, the narrator."

I force a smile, "Oh my gosh, Bink, that's awesome. That's the lead." I know from reading plays in class that the narrator always has the most lines.

"I know, crazy," Bianca says, shaking her head. "I can't believe you guys didn't get called."

I can't believe it either. Maybe Bianca's mom knows the director or something. I try to remember Bianca's audition. Was she that much better than the rest of us? I can't figure out the answer so I don't say anything for the rest of the walk to school.

Every night Jamie and I talk on the phone to rehash the day's events:

"Did you see Shawn's new haircut?"

"I talked to Robin. She likes Gabe again."

"Your new skirt is cute. Where did you get it?"

"Have you talked to Bianca?"

"No, she's at play rehearsal."

Bianca has rehearsals two nights a week and on weekends. Even though I still walk to and from school with her, I hardly know her anymore. She's missed too many phone calls and hangouts. She never mentions the play but I'm sure that's all she's thinking about. Opening night is coming up.

"I want to see it," I tell Jamie as I stretch the phone cord into my room and lean against the closed door. "I mean, even though we're not that close anymore we should go, right?"

"Yeah," Jamie says. "It's not like we're mad at her. She's still our friend."

"Totally," I say and I doodle *TOTALLY* in the margins of my pre-algebra homework. "I wonder if she's any good."

Jamie, Robin, Kim, and I get tickets to see Bianca's play on opening weekend. We show up at the same place the auditions were held but this time the theatre seems so small. I'm glad I didn't get a part: all that work and only sixty seats in the whole place? Doesn't seem worth it.

Bianca's is the first voice we hear and even though it looks like our friend, I can't believe it's her. She's so confident. She says her lines loud and clear. She's good. I can't imagine doing what she's doing and I wonder what the director saw in Bianca that told her she'd be great. Bianca's a star and I sit in my seat watching her rise above the rest of us. She scales higher up the social pyramid, and I love and hate her for it.

Home for the Holidays

We decorate the tree the first night Chet comes home for winter break. Mom tries to make it feel like Christmas even though the Nakadas and Okamotos aren't visiting this year. Usually Christmas means Dad's family driving up to ski for the holidays, but this year it's just us. I'm hanging the last of Auntie Grace's ceramic snowflakes when the phone rings. I sprint to kitchen and then pick it up on the third ring. Even though it's great to see Chet, Jamie and Kim are going to the mall to see *Gung Ho*. I don't want to see it. It will make me hate that our family is Japanese and just bought a Honda. Apparently real Americans buy American. Still, I want to hang out with my friends.

Mom's baking Christmas cookies. "Hey Mom, can I go to the mall?"

"No, Nori," she says as she sprinkles chopped nuts on a cookie sheet layered with dough. "It's Chet's first night home. We're having family time."

"Please," I whine.

"No," she says as she pulls the oven door open.

A blast of heat escapes the oven as Mom pulls one batch of cookies out and places another inside. The heat hits me as I leave the kitchen and stomp upstairs. I call Jamie to tell her I can't go. Then I slam my bedroom door for effect.

Over winter break I go skiing with Dad, Chet, Laura, and Mitch and the mountain feels empty without any aunties, uncles, or cousins. We ski Old Skyliner, Black Lift Line, and West Boundary around the Main Lodge. On our way up Red Chair Dad tells us about skiing Champaign powder in Utah and I picture Dad's smooth turns down a pristine run, a rooster tail of sparkling snow spraying behind him. I see Matt Rose, from St. Francis, and he makes fun of me because my skis aren't parallel. Luckily, I don't run into any of the Cascade boys. My ten-year-old ski gear is so embarrassing.

We go to church on Christmas Eve, and afterwards we eat Chinese food like we always do, but this year the restaurant is too cold and too quiet, just the click of chopsticks and, "Pass the rice, please." We don't order like Auntie Grace and everything tastes different. On the drive home I can tell we won't have a white Christmas. Even though it's cold enough for snow, stars light up the clear night sky.

On Christmas morning, frost crusts the ground. We open presents and then go to mass. Mom makes brunch and Jamie calls to wish me a Merry Christmas. She asks what I got (the *Pretty in Pink* soundtrack from Chet, a poster of Michael Jordan and Mars Blackman from Laura, and money from Mitch and Mom and Dad). I'm jealous because Jamie got a Swatch, Guess Jeans, and Giorgio perfume. I get off the phone as Mom starts the turkey and everyone else watches football. I'm bored. I wonder what everyone else is doing. I imagine Shawn playing football in the backyard with his dad and brothers. I glance out the window at Robin's house and picture all the great clothes she probably got. I think about calling her, but it's Christmas and I don't want to interrupt. I just hope I'm not missing anything cool while I'm stuck at home with my lame family.

On the day after Christmas Mom finally lets me go over to Jamie's house. She shows me her new Swatch and we listen to Wham! I'm so relieved to be back out in the world. I ask Jamie what's been going on and she says, "Nothing. I went with my mom to return something at the mall. No one was there. Nothing is going on. It's totally lame."

"Lame," I echo but I'm relieved I wasn't the only one stuck at home for the holidays.

"At least you have your brothers and sister," Jamie points out.

It felt so empty at our house this Christmas, but then I think about how quiet it must have been for Jamie: just her, her mom, and step-dad.

"Yeah," I shrug. "I guess my family is all right."

Setting Screens

Basketball season starts after winter break. I've been watching Chet and Laura play my whole life and played for St. Francis in the fifth grade. Dad showed me how to dribble and Chet taught me the footwork for a lay-up, so I scored almost all our team's points. I can't wait to play again, to be the point guard who brings the ball up the court, drives to the hoop, and scores or is fouled and gets to shoot free throws.

Enough seventh grade girls come out for basketball to make two teams. We stand in the gym as Ms. Wilson calls names for the green and white teams. Jamie and I link arms and hope we're together. Ms. Wilson knows how Jamie and I can get hyper, though, and she calls Jamie's name for the green team and Bianca too. I end up on the white team with Robin, but everyone else who's cool is on the green team with Valerie. Valerie's the only other one who can dribble the ball up the court so they put us on different teams.

Valerie still isn't cool. She tries to talk to me and trade papers in English class, but I'd much rather trade with Bianca or DJ Brown. She hasn't given up though and when looks at me I have to avoid all eye contact.

After setting up a few plays, the white team plays the green team, and I guard Valerie. She's pretty quick, but after she scores on me once, I figure out she only dribbles with her right hand. I steal it from her until she gets that she has to switch hands. I already dribble with my left so my team pulls ahead even though we aren't keeping score. We also win because Dayna Smith is on my team. She's new at Pilot Butte and has thick, straight brown hair, and pale skin. In our first scrimmage she catches my passes, makes a bank shot, sets screens, and rebounds better than any other seventh grader.

After practice, I'm waiting for Mom and I see Dayna leaving the gym. She has on Guess jeans, Keds, a blue parka and a scarf. She looks pretty cool.

The next day I notice Dayna in wood shop class. We talk about basketball and I ask how she likes Bend. She tells me it's okay but she liked Bellingham, Washington better. Her dad works with my dad at the Forest Service. "We should hang out sometime," I suggest.

After school on Friday I walk with Dayna to her house. It's always weird going to someone's house for the first time, but the Smith's house isn't huge, like some of the homes in Edge Cliff, so I'm not uncomfortable like I was at first at Robin and Bianca's. Dayna's mom does what we wish all moms would do: she leaves us alone. We hang out in her room where navy curtains cover the windows and a lava lamp glows in the corner. She has posters for *The Breakfast Club* and Eurhythmics. She asks me if I've ever heard of The Smiths or The Ramones as she shuffles through a collection of tapes a plastic box. I tell her I like INXS and U2.

"Cool," she says. "I bet you'd like Jane's Addiction too."

Dayna slips a tape into her boom box and I decide she's a different kind of cool. She isn't like the rest of us, but she doesn't care. She stands out in a good way. Before Dad picks me up, I tell Dayna she should start hanging out with us. Dayna gets the invitation Valerie's been trying to get all year. I set a screen that clears an open path for her into the cool group. Even though she's new, Dayna didn't try to be cool. She just figured it out, and now she's in.

Diary

I lay awake in the quiet of night. Mom and Dad's footsteps land heavily downstairs. Light seeps under my bedroom door from the hallway. I imagine Mitch sleeping in the room he used to share with Chet, and Laura finishing up homework in her room. I can't fall asleep. It's not as bad as it was a couple years ago when I worried about Mom and Dad getting a divorce. Back then my mind spun all night about family problems and the possibility of dying from leukemia. Tonight I stare out at the moon and stars as the cold night seeps through the storm window.

Mom shuts off the hall light and the house goes silent. I think about a black hole, a place of forever-dark emptiness and just as I start to lose track of time and space, her sobs begin.

I'm instantly awake. I wish Laura and I were closer. I would knock on her door and ask her what's wrong, but it's not like it was when we were little, when she taught me how to write my name in cursive and we folded origami cranes and boxes together. She helped me perfect my free throw form and showed me how to shave my legs, but now we're trapped in the silence of our family.

Maybe she's crying because she got cut from the volleyball team or because she didn't go to homecoming. Maybe she's bummed she's still wearing that big blue boot and can't play basketball for the rest of the season because the stress fracture in her foot still hasn't healed. Or maybe it's something completely different, something I know nothing about. Laura's sobs fade. Quiet returns, and I fall into the black hole of sleep.

It's a Saturday afternoon and I'm bored. I wish I could call Jamie or Robin, but Robin is on punishment and Jamie is in Portland for the weekend. I lie on my bed and study the eaves in the ceiling. I turn to my side and stare at the books on my dresser. I can't read the titles, but I know them all by size and color: *A Children's Bible, Black Beauty, Little Women, Anne of Green Gables,* classics in hardback Mom bought for Laura when she was in middle school. I've read them all.

Laura is on a band trip for the weekend but she might have something to read in her bookcase. I push her door open and light from the hallway chases me into her room. The books in the built-in are mostly familiar: *Little House on the Prairie,* Beverly Cleary's *The Mouse and the Motorcycle,* and *Beezus and Ramona.* There are a few I haven't read: *The Basketball Diaries, A Tale of Two Cities.* A book with no title. I run my fingers along the blank spine. Laura's diary.

I pull the book from the shelf and flip through page after page of my sister's neat writing. My mouth is dry, and my tongue feels thick and rough against the roof of my mouth. Laura's diary could tell me about her sobs at night. I might read about her first kiss or who she's likes. I flip to the first page: January 1984, three years ago. I count back in my head. She was in the eighth grade; I was in fourth. Back then Laura had friends over all the time. In 1984, when the phone rang it was always for Laura. That was the year Mom told me I had to leave Laura and her friends alone. I was too young. I ruined their fun.

I carry Laura's diary to my room and close the door. I sink into bed and start at the beginning. I meet my sister's best friend from middle school: Kimberly, a rich, tall, thin girl with thick auburn hair. She was beautiful and popular, and when Laura was the new girl in middle school, Kimberly befriended her. I read about rumors, lies, and ruined friendships. There are boys Laura liked, cute, popular boys, and sometimes they liked her back and sometimes they didn't. The door at the bottom of the stairs opens. I slam the diary shut, hold my breath, and wait. I shouldn't be doing this. This is a sin, the kind I would confess if I was still at St. Francis. I sneak back into Laura's room, put the diary back on the shelf, and head downstairs to watch TV.

The next day, I'm bored again. I know there's a book I want to read. I learned what Laura went through in middle school, but I still haven't uncovered the reason for her tears. She won't be back for another few hours, so I tiptoe back into her room, pull the book from the shelf, and retreat to my room again. There are huge gaps in time. Months pass with no entries. I try to keep track of time in my mind, (Laura graduates from eighth grade, she's a freshman, now a sophomore) but I lose the thread of her story. I'm almost at the end and I still have no idea why she cries at night.

When I finish reading my sister's whole diary, I close it and return it to the safety of her bookshelf, but I can't stop thinking I missed something. What happened on the days my sister wrote nothing? Why doesn't Laura hang out with Kimberly anymore? Why doesn't the phone ring? Why doesn't she have a boyfriend?

I thought I was reading so I could help my sister, but I've been reading to help myself. I want to know how my sister, who once stood atop the pyramid of popularity, toppled. Laura's diary doesn't provide me with the answers. She didn't write about how hard it can be to keep your balance on top or how she fell.

I stare back up at the eaves in my room and hate myself for invading my sister's inner world. For so long I've measured who I am against her. My success depends on how I compare to the girl she was at my age. Are my grades better than hers in middle school? Am I as popular as she was or as good at basketball?

Laura didn't have a diary to read. She didn't have an older sister to show her the way. I should do better; learn from her mistakes, but I don't know what her mistakes were. Why didn't she write about the important stuff?

I think about a confession, about telling her I read her diary. Maybe then she would tell me what changed between middle school and high school. I could ask her about her tears at night. But if she knew I'd read her diary, she would hate me. She would know the kind of person I really am: a sneaky traitor. Laura might want to help me through middle school. She might want me to stay at the top and date the cute boys, but I can't confess. She would never forgive me.

Laura gets home from her trip, and I never tell her I read her diary.

Annoying

After Bianca stars in *The Best Christmas Pageant Ever*, she tells us she's been asked to do some modeling for United Colors of Benetton in the Bend River Mall. She invites Robin and me to one of her rehearsals and the three of us ride in the Weston's Volvo to the mall. I stare at the Benetton clothes and spot several sweaters I've seen Robin and Bianca wear. Our family can't afford Benetton and even though there are Asian models in the Benetton ads, I feel out of place in this fancy store.

The owner shows us how to walk toe first down the ramp of the runway. Even though Robin and I learn to walk, Bianca's the only one they ask to be in the show. Unlike the play, none of us go see Bianca in her fashion show. I wonder how Bianca is managing to balance by herself at the top of her own cool pedestal.

Bianca writes something in English class about a mouse. Mr. Casler says it would make a great children's book. Mr. Casler's wife is a children's author and she says Bianca should publish her story. I can't believe Bink's story is that much better than all of ours. Could it really be a book? Bianca is an actress, a model *and* an author?

I write to Jamie.

JAYMI!

I'M TOTALLY BORED. ANYWAY, BC WROTE THIS STORY AND OUR MOST HATED TEACHER THINKS IT COULD BE A REAL BOOK. TOTALLY WEIRD, HUH? WRITE BACK, OKAY. LOVE YA! NOR

I reach behind me and drop the note on Jamie's desk. She reads it as Mr. Casler grades papers at his desk. We're supposed to be reading and answering the questions but Jamie reads my note and quickly passes it back to me. It has only one word in Jamie's big loopy handwriting: *Lame.*

At lunch, Bianca has to do a make-up test for Ms. Wilson so Robin, Kim, Jamie, and I discuss how Bianca's success will change her.

"She's going to get stuck up about it."

"Yeah, she already thinks she's so cool."

"So annoying."

"If she starts acting conceited we'll have to do something."

All week, we keep an eye on her.

"She was totally talking to Ezra today like she was so cool."

"So annoying."

Then on Wednesday, Bianca's absent. Being absent gives everyone time to talk about you, or forget about you. We decide Bianca's conceited. She thinks she's too cool and we can't stand it. We don't want to hang out with her anymore.

"Where were you guys this morning?" Bianca asks the next day because Robin and I didn't stop at her house that morning.

"We thought you were still sick."

"Oh, okay," Bianca says but she keeps hanging out with us even though none of us talk to her. The funny thing is, she doesn't say anything about the book or the modeling.

In English class Mr. Casler plays a movie of the story we're reading. The room is dark and Bianca passes me a note.

Hey Nor,

Mr. Casler is so stupid. Look at him. I think I'm going to quit modeling. It's lame and I never get to hang out with you guys anymore! Are you guys mad at me? Miss ya! Love ya! BC

I turn the note over and try to figure out how to respond. Maybe Bink's not so annoying after all. I dragged her with me to the play auditions, and she did try to get Robin and me into modeling. She tried to include us in her success. I write back:

BINK!

YOU SHOULD TOTALLY KEEP MODELING. IT'S SO COOL. YOU'RE SWEET!

LOVE YA, NOR

At lunch Robin whispers something into Bianca's ear. I wonder if Bianca wrote Robin a note too. I forget all about the conversation we had about Bianca not being cool. Bianca is still in, even though she was almost out. Bianca actually might be the coolest one.

A Perm, Braces and Glasses

It's a Friday afternoon when we get home from the hair salon. I stomp up the stairs and slam my bedroom door. I lean over my dresser, peer into the mirror, and I can't stop the tears from coming. I can't go out in public looking like this. First, I smell weird. That perm did something crazy to my scalp and I smell like a wet dog. I run my fingers through the mangled mess of hair. I'd been asking for a perm for months. Curly hair is cooler than my flat, fine hair. But instead of thick, glossy spiral curls my hair looks frizzy and dry. Mom's annoyed because after I begged and begged for a perm, now I hate it.

I take a deep breath and try to smile. Maybe I look awful because I'm crying, but my metal smile, all brackets and wires, makes it even worse. My eyes blur again. I'd been fine with getting the braces. Rich kids get braces and my two front teeth were so crooked I knew it would be good in the long run, but I look so different with the braces *and* a perm. I look gross. Everyone at school will stare. The boys will say disgusting things about my hair looking like pubes. People will talk behind my back.

I lay on my bed, so angry with myself for wanting this stupid perm and trying to figure out what to do to make it better. I go to the phone, dial, and stretch the cord from the hallway into my room.

"It's bad, Jamie. Really bad." I won't cry. I won't.

"I'm sure it fine."

"No. It's really bad."

"When you wash it will relax. Just wait a couple of days."

The woman at the salon told me the same thing but hearing Jamie say it makes me believe it. "You have to help me this weekend. I can't go to school like this."

I hang up the phone and calm down a little, but then I imagine Mrs. McAdams' class when I will have to wear my glasses too. I pull my glasses out of my bag and look back into the mirror.

When I first got my glasses I couldn't stop staring at the world's sharp details, the individual strands of hair on people's heads, the tiny needles on ponderosa pine trees, the clusters and berries on the junipers. But now, the glasses allow me to see my frizzy hair in even clearer detail. Braces. A perm. Glasses. I look like such a nerd. I can't possibly stay cool when I look so lame. I've become the ugly one in the group.

That's when I figure out what I have to do. I'm already the different one, the one with dark hair and olive skin. I have a Japanese dad, an adopted Korean brother, and good grades. I might as well be the Asian nerd. Everyone loves Long Duck Dong from *Sixteen Candles*, right?

On Monday, I joke about my nerdy hair, and braces, and glasses. If you make fun of yourself before anyone else, they can't hurt you. If you think of the most terrible things people might say, and say them first, you're safe. I just have to do this until the perm grows out.

At every orthodontist appointment, I ask when I can get my braces off. I start begging Mom for contact lenses. I wait for my hair to grow. When all of that happens, I won't be Long Duck Dong anymore. I'll be Nori again.

Mrs. McAdams

We're reading about the Tigris and Euphrates rivers in Mrs. McAdams' class. "You should all try to travel to the Middle East," she tells us as we look at pictures of deserts and pyramids. "They drink rose water, and eat and barley salads. Every one's skin is olive and people's eyes are dark and almond-shaped, like, like Nori's."

I sit up, surprised to hear my name in the middle of Mrs. McAdams's lecture. I hate it when she points out I'm the only one who isn't white. I know she doesn't mean to make me feel bad, but being Asian is standing out in a bad way.

We read the book, answer questions, and then choose groups to make presentations in front of the class. Bianca, Kim, and I make a group and after school Bianca and I work on a poster of Egypt's economic structure. We decide Kim has to talk since she didn't do anything for the poster.

The next day Kim acts shy and only wants to hold the poster. Bianca and I exchange a look, and we both know what to do. With Kim standing between us holding the poster it will be the ideal opportunity to pants her. Pantsing is the perfect way to get a friend, to humiliate them in a fun way. And really, with the elastic-waist shorts Kim is wearing today, she's asking for it.

That's why Bianca and I are so shocked Kim doesn't suspect our plan. We fumble through the presentation and for our finale, as soon as I finish with the words Fertile Crescent, we pull Kim's elastic shorts all the way down to her ankles.

Kim let's out a shriek and drops the poster to pull up her shorts. Bianca and I laugh. That was too easy. The whole class laughs (even Kim) and Mrs. McAdams tells Bianca and me to stay after class. Even though we get in trouble, pantsing Kim is totally worth it.

Thirteen

In the book Mom gave me about puberty and becoming a woman, it talks about *quinceañeras* in Mexico and Jewish bar mitzvahs that make it clear when you become a woman or a man. But for me, there will be no *quince* or bat mitzvah. I'm just waiting for a moment when I'll feel grown up. For girls there are bras and periods, and for boys a voice change. When Gabe, Jason, or Cougar call my family teases me about a boy on the phone. Even though I wear a bra and have my period every month, I still feel like a kid. Maybe on my thirteenth birthday I'll feel grown up.

Mom drives toward downtown to run errands. The Cascades shine white against a cold blue sky. "So, what do you want to do for your birthday this year?" she asks.

I remember last year when the worlds of my friends collided. I don't want that again. We cross the Deschutes River. Freezing cold water crashes over rocks and flows under the bridge.

"Well, if you could do anything, and money didn't matter, what would you want?" Mom prods again.

I look at the black river water surrounded by a landscape of brown grass and naked tree limbs. "I'd take everyone to Hawaii." I imagine warm, blue waves, and palm trees blowing in a tropical paradise.

Mom shifts the car to next gear. "Well, we could go to Kahneeta. They have a pool and the water is warm from the hot spring. Maybe we'll get lucky and it will be a nice day."

I can't remember the pool on the Warm Springs Indian Reservation but I know I've been there from pictures. I was really little, and it was before Mitch came. Chet and Laura splashed in the shallow end, and I teetered along the edge of the pool. In the background, big brown bear sculptures sprayed water.

I calculate the amount of fun a Kahneeta birthday would be but worry about all of the unknowns: Who would go? Would the fickle weather cooperate? Would Mom leave us alone? I picture my friends lying out in the sun, looking cool. "Sure," I say as Mom turns into the post office. "Sounds fun."

Kim and Robin are out of town the day of my birthday party so I invite Stephanie Troutman and Dayna along with Bianca and Jamie. We drive north on highway 97 on a perfect spring day. We cross the Crooked River Gorge and I forget not to look down into the canyon. The steep, sheer cliffs fall toward a thin blue ribbon of water that always makes my stomach drop. I push away the feeling of ghosts and try not to think about all the people who have committed suicide here. Instead, I think about my birthday. I look up at the blue sky and let the ghosts of the Gorge fade behind me.

We drive through Madras onto the Warm Springs Reservation and by the time we reach the resort the sun towers high above us. Mom pays our admission and we go off by ourselves. We lay our towels on the pool deck across from the bear statues spraying water into the air. It's warm so we strip off shorts and sweatshirts, and pull towels and magazines out of our bags. We soak up the sun and snap pictures. We pose like models in front of the pool, our thin arms hanging around one another's shoulders and I feel grown up. The afternoon speeds by, and before we know it, it's time to meet Mom at the car. On the drive home, we're a little bit tan from our day in the weak sunshine, and I fall asleep on Bianca's shoulder.

A few days later, I get the film back from Rexall. I study the pictures of my girlfriends and me. Our legs are so long and skinny, and none of us really fill the tops of our swimsuits. Even though I felt so grown up that day, in the photos we still look like little girls. I'm not a woman yet, but at least I'm a teenager. Thirteen doesn't mean I'm grown up, but I'm closer.

Getting Ready

Daylight savings time ends and when Robin, Bianca, and I walk to school the sun is already up. Spring is close and as soon as the afternoon highs reach the 50s, we wear shorts and tank tops revealing pale skin long hidden under sweaters and jeans.

The Friday of the spring dance, Kim and Jamie come over to get ready. We watch one another closely and check out what we've chosen to wear: surf company t-shirts, shorts and sandals. We thread together leis from the crabapple tree blossoms in the front yard. We brush our hair, curl, and spray. I blow-dry my hair and the perm is barely noticeable. We apply deodorant, lotion, and perfume. By the time we're ready to go we are three variations of the same look and smell: shoulder length hair, curled and sprayed, lip gloss, shorts, t-shirts, sandals, and flower leis: perfect for Spring Dance.

Mom drops us off at school, and we can't wait for Prince's "U Got the Look" and Billy Idol's "Mony Mony." Our leis fall to pieces, just white petals drifting to the floor, but we don't care. The eighth graders dance in their circle and we dance in ours. I keep an eye on Shawn. He and Caren finally broke up, and maybe if I'm around during a slow song he'll ask me to dance. But when they play "Take My Breath Away" Shawn leaves, so I head to the bathroom, hoping I might bump into him. I time it perfectly, and we almost collide at the door.

"Cool sunglasses," I say as I pull them from his face. "Oooh. Varnets. Can I borrow?"

"Uh," before he can answer I walk off with his glasses and wear them for the rest of the night.

It's almost 9:00. The dance is almost over. U2's "With or Without You" comes on and Shawn comes up to me.

Oh my god, oh my god, oh my god.

He looks uncomfortable and won't look me in the eye.

"Uh, hey Nori," he says, turning to look over his shoulder.

I can't believe he's right there, standing right there in front of me. He reaches out a hand. I smile and look at my feet.

"Can I get my sunglasses back?"

First Kiss

The clock is ticking.

Robin had her first kiss with Gabe when they went out.

Bianca had her first kiss with Peter Moore.

Kim kissed Chris Rexrode at the spring dance.

Pecks from Jimmy Olson in fifth grade and Todd Hoffman during Spin the Bottle don't count. I know who I want to be my first real kiss, but Shawn hasn't talked to me since he asked for his sunglasses back. I wouldn't be surprised if he and Caren are back together. Even though I smile at him everyday in choir, he hardly notices me.

Jamie's first kiss isn't happening anytime soon either. She doesn't like Dally anymore. Now she likes Gabe (like every other girl in school), but he told me the other day he doesn't like anyone.

Jamie and I sit on her waterbed on a bright blue Saturday afternoon. Even though there's still ice on the ground, spring is here. We flip through prom issues of our favorite magazines, as Crowded House plays in the tape deck, "Hey now, hey now, don't dream it's over." We read articles about how to tease our hair perfectly, how to make our perfume last all day, and which bras will catch our crush's eye. Then it's: "First Date Horror Stories" and "How Do You Know He Loves You?" but the article that keeps us busy for most of the afternoon is "Stealing His Heart With Just One Kiss."

Jamie and I both know what we need to do to keep up. We have to go out with someone and experience our first kiss in order to stay cool. We practice on our forearms, parting our lips and sneaking in a little tongue but not too much just like the article says. By the end of the afternoon we're both ready. Our lips are soft and our breath is minty. We close our eyes and imagine fingers brushing a cheek, a palm pressing on the small of the back or gently caressing the base of the neck. Our first kisses will be passionate and perfect.

A few weeks later, Travis Smith asks me out. He's an eighth grader, and he's on Mitch's baseball team. He has red hair and freckles and I convince myself he's cute. I mostly go out with him because the clock is ticking and everyone knows eighth grade boys expect to kiss.

Travis comes over to hang out with Mitch after school and Kim comes over too. Mom has a "no friends in the house unless parents are home" rule so we have to find something to do outside. Mitch and Travis play catch in the backyard while Kim and I sit on the front steps. Laura comes home, parks, and heads inside. She leaves the car unlocked, and the wind is picking up so Kim and I sit in the warm bucket seats of my sister's Datsun 210.

"Want me to go get Travis?" Kim asks as she plays with a window scraper, an Amy Grant tape, and a handful of Taco Bell hot sauce packets from the glove compartment.

I fidget with the gearshift. "Sure, I guess."

"I'm going to tell him to kiss you."

The sun shines through the windows heating the car. My palms are dry, and my breath is minty from my gum. I know I need to do this. I'm ready, but I'm nervous. I shrug.

Kim flings the door open, and as I wait I know this could be my moment, my first real kiss; the one I'll remember for the rest of my life. The car windows are dingy and Laura's car always smells like syrup. Travis comes around the corner, and I look over my shoulder to make sure Mom isn't pulling up. Travis climbs in on the passenger side, and even though we're going out we've hardly talked.

"Hey," he says. His voice is deep and I remember he's a bass in choir.

I smile and look up at him. He reaches out for my hand. Thank God it's not sweaty.

He pulls me toward him. I lean over the stiff parking brake and see his freckled face coming toward mine. I close my eyes like I'm supposed to and he is there, hot breath and lips on mine. But his lips are too wet, and suddenly his tongue is in my mouth and I can hardly breath. It feels so strange and wet and slimy compared to when I practiced on my arm.

I let him kiss me for a few seconds and then push his tongue out of my mouth because it's moving too fast. His hands grip my shoulders tight and my heart pounds. I don't know if it's the heat of passion or the sun shining through the car windows making me sweat. All I smell is burnt, dusty syrup and Travis is still there, right in my face.

I have to get out of that car. I pull away, wipe my spitty mouth on the sleeve of my sweatshirt, and bolt out of the car slamming the door behind me.

Kim and Mitch are in the back yard shooting hoops. I tell Mitch I think Travis is ready to go home.

"Did you do it?" Kim asks.

I nod and grin even though I'm grossed out. At least I got my first kiss over with.

The next day, during lunch, Kim tells Travis I'm breaking up. I can't imagine kissing him again, and I can't believe I'll forever be connected to Travis Smith as my first kiss.

Bianca and I walk home after school. "So, how was it?" she asks and I know she means the kiss.

I shrug. I don't know if I can tell Bianca that it wasn't anything like I imagined. "It was okay, kind of slimy."

Bianca laughs. "Then he wasn't a very good kisser."

"I guess not."

Bianca says bye and heads into her house.

I walk slowly toward home as birds chirp above me. The clock that had been ticking for my first kiss has stopped. I walk in the bright sunlight and know I'm keeping up. As I walk past the field, Mom pulls into the driveway, and I meet her in the garage.

"Hi, Nori," she says as she closes the car door and hands me couple of bags of groceries. "How was your day?"

I force a smile and grab the bags. I wonder if she can tell I've had my first kiss. Can she tell I've gone out with a boy, kissed him and broken up with him all in the course of three days? "It was all right." I follow her up the garage steps and into the house.

"Just all right?"

"Yep," I add as I close the garage door behind me. "Just all right."

The door seals shut behind me, closing on the girl I am at school. At Pilot Butte I'm Nori Nakada who hangs out with the popular girls and kissed Travis Smith. Mom doesn't know that girl at all. She still sees her baby, Chet, Laura and Mitch's little sister, a girl with good grades who talks on the phone too much. I'm the one she doesn't need to worry about. Mom doesn't care about my friends, or school, or boys even though that's all I think about. She thinks about Chet away at college, Laura's stress fracture, Mitch's grades, and marriage counseling. She has no idea her baby just experienced her first kiss.

"Anything else?" I ask. I can still be the girl Mom thinks I am.

Mom starts putting groceries away. "No, Honey. I got it."

I head upstairs. Instead of talking to Mom I call Jamie. We have to talk about everything that happened today.

Spring Fever

Spring is here and while life at home goes on as usual, things at Pilot Butte have turned giddy, like a few hundred chipmunks set loose after being cooped up all winter. Cougar asks me out and I say yes, but it's weird because we've known each other since second grade. The one time we kiss it feels like kissing my brother. We break up after a couple of days.

At the end of the year dance, DJ Brown and I slow dance three times and I figure he's going to ask me out, but he never calls. On Monday it's weird between us and we usually joke around. I figure he doesn't want to mess up our friendship.

At break, I hear John Eby likes me. John is cute. He has a hot tan from track and baseball and unlike Cougar and DJ, who I've known forever, I have no history with John.

I tell Jamie I think I like John. Jamie tells Robin who tells Melissa Jacobson who tells Joe Speck who is friends with John and pretty soon word gets back to me that John is going to ask me out.

At lunch I sit at my usual table and Joe walks over. I've known Joe for years, but he's shy so I know this is killing him. I try to make it easy for him. "Hey, Joe. How's it going?" I act casual even though I know why he's here.

"I'm fine." Joe's voice has changed. He sounds grown up. "So, you know John," Joe looks back toward his table where John talks with Chad Davidson.

I glance at the table. "Yeah," I say and then lower my eyes. Obviously, I know him.

"Well, he wants to know if you wanna go out."

I shrug and hope Joe doesn't tell John how red my face got when he asked me. "Sure."

"Cool," Joe says and he walks back to his table. He talks to John. John looks over and smiles right at me. Knowing his perfect white smile is for me makes me warm all over. I smile back and Jamie and Kim both yell, "Ooooh," as I bury my head in my arms. When I look back up John has left the cafeteria.

Track is over, so with no sports after school and Mom and Dad still at work I'm in no hurry to go home. John and I plan to hang out after school. We meet out behind the wood shop and I hope he'll kiss me. Maybe this time it will be different.

We hike up the slope behind D Hall. We're alone, but I can hear the faint voices of our friends in the distance. We sit next to one another on the warm, pine needle covered ground. Our knees and elbows touch and then don't touch, touch, don't touch. He's so quiet and I wonder if this is ever going to happen. He puts his arm around me and I can smell his warm berry bubblegum breath. The sun shines bright through the juniper and pine trees. He leans into me and moves so slowly, so smoothly, I have time to breathe, close my eyes, and push my gum to the side of my mouth. We kiss softly in the bright dark of eyes closed on a sunny day. He holds my face in his warm hands and the whole world slows down. Birds chirp above us and the voices of our friends drift through the trees. Warmth spreads through me, like my insides are made of warm chocolate chip cookies right from the oven.

Bianca calls my name and it echoes through the quiet. I open my eyes and John is still there. He smiles and we both laugh. "I have to go," I say and we walk down the slope saying nothing, just smiling and holding hands.

John and I never have another chance to hang out again, so even though we go out for almost two weeks, we never kiss again. I break up with him on the second-to-last day of school. He'll be away all summer so we'll never see one another. Still, I know whenever I see him, I'm going to remember that kiss.

My first kiss: Travis Smith. My second kiss: Cougar Caverhill. My third kiss: John Eby. It's a good thing no one's keeping track. Mom would be horrified.

Elections

Jamie and I can't wait for eighth grade. We'll go to all the dances and be in student council. We'll say the announcements together every morning and be goofy on the loud speaker just like we are when we share in Miss Wilson's class. We will play all the sports and have boyfriends, or maybe not, because it won't matter. We'll be popular, and it'll be the best.

Step one for our vision is winning student body elections. Jamie runs for president and I run for vice president. She is the confident, blonde extrovert. I'm the short, sassy brunette.

I run unopposed, but Kim runs against Jamie. I don't think it will matter. Kim is popular, but she isn't always nice. Besides, everyone knows Jamie and I go together. We read our speeches from the cafeteria stage before everyone votes and all afternoon we wait to hear the results. During Mrs. McAdams' class, Mr. Mero finally gets on the PA and congratulates the candidates. The classroom grows quite and I hear, "Brooke Uffleman is your class treasurer, Erin Steffy is your secretary, Nori Nakada is your Vice President, and your president for the 1987-1988 school year is..."

I close my eyes, hoping he'll say Jamie Richards, but instead I hear, "Kim Mitchell."

Kim smiles on the other side of the classroom and Bianca hugs her. I skip over to congratulate her, but I'm thinking of Jamie. She's in science right now, and I imagine her face getting red. I hope she doesn't cry. The bell rings, and I hurry to catch Jamie before she leaves, but she's not at her locker or in front of school.

"Hey, good job, Nori. Way to go Bink," seventh and eighth graders say as Bianca and I leave campus together.

When I get home I call Jamie. She acts like it's not a big deal, but I know we're both devastated. Eighth grade might not be how we imagined.

Out

For two mornings in a row Robin is sick. We don't walk to school together and I wonder what's going on with her. Bianca calls to find out and Robin says something about having cancer. Robin tells Bink not to tell anyone but everyone knows Bink can't keep a secret.

"Could she die?" I ask when Bianca tells me. I'm thinking about Bethy Hurley and Wendy Fouts. They both died of cancer.

"I don't know," Bianca answers.

I want to call Robin, but I'm not supposed to know, so I call Jamie while Bianca calls Kim. It's phone call crazy because we can't believe Robin might die.

Bianca eventually tells her mom, and her mom calls to see if there's anything she can do. Robin's mom tells Mrs. Weston Robin doesn't have cancer. She has an infection.

At first there is relief (thank God Robin isn't going to die) but then we're mad. How could Robin lie about something so serious? We were all worried, but now we want to confront her about her lie.

Robin doesn't come to school the next day giving us all more time to talk more about what happened.

"Cancer isn't a joke."

"I know. How could she lie like that?"

"She just wants attention."

Robin isn't at school the next day so her lie has time to spread like a cancer left untreated. It grows into every lie Robin has ever told.

"Sometimes, when Robin talks she spits and I'm all like, 'The news, please, not the weather.'"

"And it's totally gross when she gets food stuck in her braces."

"And what's with all those pictures of that yogi her parents have all over their house? What are they, Rajneeshees or something?"

"And she's always talking about people behind their back."

By Friday, we convince Kim to call Robin and they end up yelling at one another. Then Robin's mom calls Kim's mom and Kim ends up on punishment for the whole weekend.

It's the second to last day of school and Robin's still absent. On the way to school Bianca and I try to figure out what to do.

"She needs to know she can't lie about things like that."

"She shouldn't lie at all."

"I know. We totally have to talk to her."

"I know. Totally."

After school Bianca and Kim come over and we call Robin, but she won't pick up the phone. The three of us walk across the street and make our way around to the back door so Robin's mom won't see us.

Bianca taps on the sliding glass door, and Robin comes out on the wide back porch with her arms crossed across her chest. She doesn't smile. None of us do. We stand in the shade of a huge ponderosa pine, waiting.

Bianca asks why she lied.

Robin doesn't say anything.

I ask why she's missed all these days of school.

Kim wants to know why she hasn't called to talk about what happened.

"I've been really sick."

"We need to talk this out."

"When you don't come to school it makes things worse."

"You can't ignore us forever."

Robin starts to cry.

I rewind the conversation and try to figure out where it went wrong. Why is she so upset? We're all friends. We've been friends since I started at Pilot Butte, through the good times and bad. Robin was my connection to the cool kids; we've gone to movies, and ice-skating, and to all the school dances. Doesn't she want to be friends anymore? Doesn't she know that if she turns her back on us it would be over for her?

"I can't believe you're ganging up on me like this," Robin stammers. "I don't have to talk to you guys. I'm going inside."

"We're not ganging up on you," Bianca and I say in unison which sounds a lot like ganging up.

"We just want to talk it out," I add.

"Well, I don't."

Robin disappears into the TV room where we used to watch *Days of Our Lives* every afternoon. She slides the door shut behind her.

Bianca, Kim, and I walk away. We've had fights before but this feels different. I try to figure out how it came to this. I look over my shoulder at Robin's house and calculate how one lie got so out of hand. I wonder if we'll fix this or if I'll ever set foot in Robin's house again. All I know is I won't be walking with Robin on the last day of seventh grade.

Last Day

On the last day of school I look over at Robin's house. I could just cross the street, walk up to the front door, and tell her to come to school, but I don't. I head down Jones Road unsure who is to blame for everything with Robin. When I get to Bianca's house it's just like it's been for the last week and a half.

"Hi, Mrs. Weston."

"Still no Robin?"

"Still no Robin."

Bianca comes downstairs and we head off to school.

It's the finale of the Jamie and Nori show in Ms. Wilson's pre-algebra class. We planned on singing "No One Is to Blame" by Howard Jones. We each bring a tennis racket to be our air guitars but we forget a boom box so our finale becomes a slightly flat acapella version of us singing,

"You can look at the menu but you just can't eat, you can feel the cushions but you can't have a seat, you can dip your foot in the pool but you can't have a swim, you can feel the punishment but you can't feel the sin, and you want her, and she wants you, no one, no one, no one, is to blame, dunt, dunt dunt."

I'm not thinking about who is to blame for Robin anymore. I don't think about the lyrics at all.

We carry around yearbooks and throw papers and notebooks into the round metal trashcans at the ends of the halls. Loretta and I clean out our locker and I give her a hug. We're friends again and even though it will never be like it was in elementary it's better.

At lunch we watch the eighth graders hug and cry. I can't understand why they're being so dramatic. It's not like someone died. It's not like you're never going to see these people again.

Then I think about Robin. Maybe the sick feeling I have in my stomach about Robin is what the eighth graders are feeling. Maybe that's how I'll feel a year from now.

After lunch I go to choir. It's my last class with Shawn. Even though I've gone out with Travis, Cougar, and John seventh grade was about my crush on Shawn. I stare at the back of his head and wish things had been different. I guess it wasn't meant to be. Maybe in a couple of years, when we're both in high school, we'll be together.

We sing "Kyrie" one last time. Loretta and the sopranos start, I come in with the altos, and Shawn's voice joins in with the basses. We sing through the last movement and as the chord resolves I get chills.

Sixth grade was fun, seventh grade even better, but I can't wait for eighth grade. Just on the other side of summer vacation we will be back, and this will be the best summer ever. Eighth grade is going to rock. I can feel it.

Slumber Party

On the first night of summer Bianca has a slumber party. Her parents built a fort, a kind of clubhouse, next to their house where we can hangout away from adults. It also makes sneaking out to meet the boys who are sleeping over at Jason Davis' house super easy.

Bianca's mom is always particular about how many people Bianca invites to things and this time, because Robin's not there, it's Kim, Jamie, Darcy, Loretta, and me. No one mentions Robin even though she and Bianca have been friends for so long. It's almost as if she's dead. When Wendy Fouts died, though, we went to the counselor to talk about how sad and scared we felt, but Robin doesn't get any of that. We just stop talking about her as if she was never here.

We roll out our sleeping bags and listen to The Beastie Boys and Def Leopard. We talk about the boys who are at Jason's: Gabe, Cody, and Cougar, and wait for night to fall. Then we watch for the lights in the house to go out. When we think it's safe, we climb down the ladder one by one.

The night air is cool as we sprint across the driveway where freedom awaits us, but a light flips on in the house projecting a square of light onto the pavement.

We freeze, wait, and hold our breath.

The light flips back off and we sprint back to the fort, pushing one another up the ladder as quickly as we can, sliding into our sleeping bags, and feigning sleep just in case Bianca's mom comes out to check on us.

After a few tense minutes, the risk of being caught fades away, and we laugh. We wonder if the boys are out there and enjoy the idea of them waiting for us in the dark beneath the starry summer sky.

Darcy just got braces a couple days ago and even though she was hoping to kiss Jason tonight she thinks it's going to be weird. "What if our braces get stuck or something? That would suck."

"I've never kissed someone who had braces," I say.

Kim thinks back through the boys she's kissed. "Me neither."

"Do you really think you could get stuck together?"

That's when Bianca comes up with a brilliant plan. Even though we aren't playing truth or dare she says, "I dare Nori and Kim to see if you can hook braces."

"I'm not kissing her," I say.

"You don't have to kiss. Just see what happens if you touch braces."

Kim and I sit across from one another cross-legged, pulling our lips back from our teeth. I can't stop giggling and neither can Kim. We move our faces closer and closer, and then Bianca pushes me and Jamie pushes Kim and our teeth smack together. For a second we are stuck and I can smell Kim. She smells like strawberries. We both pull away and I hear a zipping sound. We were stuck and now we aren't, but somehow Kim pulled the wire out from my braces.

"My mom is going to kill me," I say but no one hears me because everyone's laughing so hard.

Kim's braces are fine and she hands me the thin wire that used to connect my braces. I shake my head knowing I can't make a big deal out of this or I'll look lame. I throw the wire away and wonder what Mom is going to say. I'll just tell her Kim and I got pushed into one another and got stuck. It sounds ridiculous, but it's the truth and Mom hates liars. Besides, no lie could possibly make this better.

Crowded House

Jamie and I have listened to her Crowded House tape so many times we know every word by heart. They play "Something So Strong" and "Don't Dream It's Over" on the radio but we know every line in "Mean to Mean," "Hole in the River," and "That's What I Call Love" too. We balance on her waterbed and sing at the top of our lungs from imaginary microphones. We love Crowded House, but no one else knows how amazing they are. Their songs match exactly how we feel about life and love.

"Hey now, hey now, don't dream it's over..."

"Love can make you weep, can make you run for cover."

Crowded House is playing at the Oregon State Fair in Salem and after begging our parents Jamie's step-dad agrees to drive us over the Santiam Pass on his day off.

On a cool morning, Jamie and I pile into the back of her dad's pick-up. It's the same week Gabe calls Jamie for the first time so she's hyper. We lay quilts in the truck bed, eat Cool Ranch Doritos and Skittles, drink Pepsi, and listen to Crowded House. Two hours later we pull into the State Fair parking lot. There are thousands of people and I don't know how we'll meet up with Bianca and her friend Emily.

The concert is the last of the night, so we explore the smelly animal stands, eat corndogs, and ride the Zipper before lining up for the show. We spot Bink and Emily in line and take turns saving a spot. It's hot, and there's hardly any shade. We drink Pepsi and lemonade, and it grosses me out that I haven't had to pee all day. We buy Crowded House concert t-shirts and change into them. They are the coolest t-shirts ever.

The sun hangs heavily in the sky and when it finally starts to fall they open the gates to the amphitheatre. We run to the open seating in the front of the flat black stage cluttered with instruments gleaming in the late afternoon heat.

We wait and wait until suddenly they are there, on stage, right in front of us. This band all the way from Australia, the one we've been singing with all summer is right there. We scream just like the black and white footage of girls going crazy for Elvis or The Beatles. I look around at the thousands of people but I'm sure Jamie and I are Crowded House's biggest fans. We jump up and down, scream, and hope they'll see us and know how much we love them.

I can tell by the first few drum beats that they're playing "Love You 'Til the Day I Die." We bob to the beat and sing, "Outside the window pane, the sound of pouring rain, all makes me glad of you. When I am far away, I am always with you." We smile, dance, and sing and a couple of times Nick looks right at me. He makes eye contact and smiles at *me*.

We sing, "Hey now, hey now, don't dream it's over" during the encore and I don't want this night to ever end. It's my first concert with my best friends and my favorite band playing into the fading summer light. I want to bottle this feeling up, but the band finishes and the stage goes dark. The house lights come on and it's over. We hug Bianca and Emily goodbye, and Jamie and I climb back into the truck. We head back over the mountain toward home.

Summer Loss

Through the warm, bright light of sleep on a July morning a ring enters the fog of my dreams. Tennis lessons are over so I know it's okay I'm sleeping in. Sometimes Jamie, Kim, or Gabe call early, but I'm still in bed. I don't get up to answer. Someone downstairs picks up. No one yells for me, so I drift back to sleep. I don't hear Mom's footsteps up the stairs, but feel her weight sink onto the bed as she lays a gentle hand on my shoulder. "There's been an accident," she says and it takes a minute for me to focus my eyes on her. I turn my eyes toward the dark space beneath the long dresser against the wall. Before my mind can spin through the possibilities she says, "Wendy Sheerer died in a car crash on Butler Market Road last night. Isn't that Gabe's sister?"

I nod and Mom says she's sorry before she leaves. I shift my head to a cooler part of the pillow. Should I call Gabe, or ride my bike out to his house to tell him I'm sorry? I remember what happened in our house the spring Chet's best friend Greg Bob was killed. The air became cold and thick and everyone moved in slow motion like we were underwater. I can't imagine the phone ringing into that kind of silence at Gabe's house or entering into their dark living room with nothing to say. I pull my heavy body into the hall to call Jamie but the phone rings. It's Kim.

"Did you hear?"

"Yeah," I say and my voice is still quiet with sleep.

We both wonder how Gabe is doing but are too scared to call. Kim asks if I still want to go to the coast with her. I can't even think about it. With one phone call everything has changed.

I call Jamie. Gabe was about to ask her out, but who knows what will happen now. When I tell her the news she starts to cry. She says she'll ride her bike over.

I wish I could tell Bianca but she's at horse camp and then I remember Robin. Robin and Gabe went out for the longest last year and I wonder if she's heard. Wendy's death is so much bigger than our stupid fight. I can't even remember what that fight was about. I want to talk to her even though I haven't seen her since the day we confronted her on her back porch.

I walk out the front door and the sunlight shocks my eyes. Before I cross the street, I stop. I'm scared to cross the road. The length of her driveway seems too far to cross on my own. Jamie will be here soon. I'll wait. I turn back around and walk back inside.

Jamie and I hang out in my room and talk about the accident. I turn off the radio. Madonna is completely wrong for today. I ask Jamie if we should go talk to Robin.

"Maybe it will make things better," Jamie says, so we walk the hundred yards between my front door and Robin's.

I knock on the side door by their breakfast room and Robin's Mom answers. I know how she feels about us. She thinks we're bullies. I want to tell her that if Robin would just talk to us, things could be better. Instead I ask if Robin's home.

She shuts the door without saying anything and Jamie and I stand there for a minute, wondering what we should do. Jamie turns to walk away but then the door opens again and Robin is there, filling the doorway. Her little sister and Mom stand behind her.

"What do you guys want?" she asks without looking at us.

"Did you hear about Gabe's sister?" I ask.

Robin nods, "Of course, my sister's in her grade."

I don't know what to say. "Well," I look at Jamie but she's messing with the pine needles on the driveway. "Well, I know you guys were close and I guess I just wanted to make sure you're okay."

Robin finally looks at me and it feels like we're in a staring contest. "I'm fine."

"Well, we could hang out if you want, you know, and talk about it." When I say *it* I mean so much more than the accident. I hope Robin knows that.

Robin stares again. She hates me. "No," she says. "You should go."

I turn and join Jamie who is already heading down the driveway. We walk away and decide that was a stupid idea.

Dayna calls that night and tells me the funeral's Friday. She asks if I'll go with her and I say I'll call her back. I head downstairs. Mom's in the kitchen wiping down the counters.

"Do you want to go?" Mom asks.

"I think I should go for Gabe."

"Well, then you need to call Kim and tell her you aren't going to the coast."

"But I want to go to the coast too," I tell Mom as I doodle on the bottom of her grocery list. Kim's family invited me to spend the weekend with them at the coast. I picture a funeral service: Gabe and his parents looking pale and shocked the same way the Hurleys looked at Bethy's funeral two summers ago. Instead of Gabe with a tan from fishing, a crooked smile, and light brown hair he will be shocked with grief. If I don't go to the service I won't have that image in my mind.

I wish Mom would tell me what to do but instead she says, "It's up to you, Nori."

I call Kim. She really wants me to go with her. "My mom won't let me go to the funeral anyway. I promise it will be fun, Nor. It will be good to get away."

Jamie's mom doesn't let her go because she's never been to a funeral and Bianca's still out of town. So while Kim and I drive to the coast, Dayna goes to the service by herself.

I never say anything to Gabe about what happened. It's just like all the things my family never mentions. It's like the quiet that stretches from my house to Robin's. I never say a thing to Gabe. Sometimes silence is all I know.

Back to School

We drive the car and Dad's truck filled with Chet's stuff to Eugene. He's starting his second year at the University of Oregon as a resident adviser. Last year Mom was so worried about him going away to school but he did great and this year he'll be helping freshmen adjust to college life.

We unpack the car as students stroll down sidewalks and green lawns. Couples walk with arms draped around shoulders and groups of friends toss hacky sacks and Frisbees.

I imagine how it will be when I go away to college. Jamie and I will be roommates, but we won't go to the University of Oregon. I want to get on an airplane when I go to college. I've never been on a plane, but I want to fly away to Harvard or Georgetown. Then I'll go to law school because lawyers make money, and I'm tired of being poor. Besides, lawyers are smart and sometimes they go on to be governors, senators, or even the president.

I unload the last box from the car and check out Chet's room. Oregon is great for Chet, but when I picture myself at college I see an east coast campus where fall colors accent old brick buildings and towering trees. Or it will be a campus in California, Long Beach State or Stanford, where I'll play for a National Championship women's basketball team. Then I'll move east for law school. I have no idea how to get there, but that's my plan, for sure.

Extended Summer

Jamie and I can't wait for the first day of school. We plan our first day of school outfits and I want to wear my Crowded House shirt but Jamie thinks Bianca is wearing hers. The last thing I want is to show up in the same shirt as someone else. I decide on cut-off jeans and a faded grey t-shirt. It's a perfect I-don't-care-that-it's-the-first-day-of-school outfit. Jamie chooses a red and white striped Esprit tank dress she got in California over the summer.

But Bend is having some kind of a budget crisis so they push back the start of school. All summer we've been waiting and now we have to wait a little longer. With a few extra days, Jamie and I decide we have to do something fun. Something crazy. We pull on our swimsuits and ride our bikes up to Taco Bell for lunch. Then we dip our feet in the fountain at the Medical Plaza down the block, but it's too quiet and on the last day of summer. We have to go big.

The Bend sign. On Highway 97 there is a landscaped divide spelling out BEND in flowers.

"Let's ride over there and lay out, you on one side, me on the other," Jamie says.

"Sure," I say with a shrug.

We take as many side streets as we can and then cross the highway at the light by the Riverhouse. The grass at the Bend sign is perfect and Jamie and I can't believe we're doing this. My heart pounds as cars and semi-trucks speed past. I lay my towel on the near side and Jamie sprints to the other side. I recline for a minute but I can't see Jamie. Traffic whizzes by and cars honk at the two crazy girls lying out on the Bend sign. The fumes start to make me dizzy and this isn't nearly as fun as I thought it would be. I sit up and yell, "This is lame" but Jamie can't hear me over the traffic, so I motion for her to come over. She picks up her towel and heads back. We pull on our t-shirts and shorts, shove our towels in my backpack and get back on our bikes.

We ride home on this last day of summer as the sun starts to set. It's been a summer of bike rides and tennis, movies, suntans, concerts, and death. Now it's over. Eighth grade is finally here. At the corner of Jones Road and Eighth Street we say goodbye just like Gordy and Chris do at the end of *Stand By Me*.

"I'll see ya."

"Not if I see you first."

Eighth Grade

The First Day of the Rest of Your Life

On the morning of the first day of school I stand in front of the full-length mirror in Mom and Dad's room and stare at my cut offs, grey t-shirt and Stan Smiths. My woven tote bag packed with new school supplies hangs from my shoulder. The perm is finally gone, so my hair falls in a perfect bob, and Dr. Quaz promises I'll be getting my braces off before picture day. I stare at my reflection and almost feel cute.

I head out the door and glance across the street toward Robin's house. Her bedroom light is off. Jamie's mom saw Robin's mom at the bank and found out Robin is going to Sunriver Prep. I wish I could tell Robin to just come back to Pilot Butte, that everything would be okay, but it's too late. I head down Jones Road alone, kicking a pinecone the whole way.

When I pick up Bianca, she shakes her head. "I can't believe Robin's gone."

"I know. It's really weird."

That's all we say about it.

The thing I'm most excited about on the first day is that Kim and I, as president and VP, get to do the morning announcements. We show up in the main office and I already have it planned out. We saw *Good Morning Vietnam* a couple of weeks ago and I want to start the announcements the way Robin Williams did for the troops. Kim is suddenly shy. She stands next to me but refuses to say a word.

My hands shake when I click on the microphone and yell, "Goooooood Moooooorning Pilot Butte," I imagine laughter from my classmates, but the office is too far from any classes for me to know how everyone's reacting. I read through the rest of the announcements and worry that instead of laughing with me everyone's laughing at me.

I walk to my first period class and see DJ Brown taking the attendance to the office. Last year DJ gave me feedback when

Jamie and I shared in math so I ask, "What did you think?"

"Well," he smiles, "you definitely got people's attention." He keeps walking.

I head to class knowing I'll never start the announcements like that again.

The first day of school is boring. We sit at the eighth grade tables in the cafeteria and find out everyone's locker locations and schedules. Teachers go over rules and I already know I don't like Mr. Hess and Mrs. Whitworth is my favorite.

In Ensemble, I sit next to Bianca and Gabe is there. He looks okay. He doesn't look wrecked with grief like I feared. I still feel bad I wasn't at the funeral. I smile in his direction and he smiles back. We've hardly talked since his sister's accident and although he seems a little sad around the edges he seems basically the same.

Jamie and I only have leadership together but we share a locker so we see one another each passing period. I'm waiting for her after school when Dayna comes by. "Have you heard?"

I shake my head.

"Jamie went home early. She started her period."

"Oh no," I imagine a wide swath of red bleeding across her red and white striped Esprit dress. "Was it bad?"

Dayna doesn't say anything but raises her eyebrows.

When I get home Mom asks about my first day. I don't know what to say. The brainpower I once used for school is now focused on popularity studies and relationship equations. I don't want to tell Mom about Gabe looking okay, or Jamie's accident. "It was okay," I say and Mom continues putting away dishes from the washer.

I need to call Jamie so I head up to my room. "Oh my gosh, what happened?"

She doesn't want to talk about it. "I just want to forget it ever happened."

I hang up the phone and can't believe this is how eighth grade is starting.

Soccer Practice

I chug down a glass of water and pull on cleats and shin guards for soccer practice at Ponderosa Park. Dad drives down Bear Creek Road toward the soccer field as I think about everything that's happened this first week of school. Everyone forgets about Jamie's accident after Gabe asks her out and they are a perfect couple. Bianca and Jason Davis start going out too.

We get to the soccer field and I run across the short-clipped grass. I forget about school for a couple of hours. I'm the only girl on the team, but I can still beat most of the boys in sprints. We stretch in the fading light and it's nice spending time with the girl I was before I went to Pilot Butte. Here, I'm still the girl who plays soccer and basketball, dodge ball and kickball. Now I play most of the sports with other girls, but there's no girls' soccer in Bend, so I have to play with the boys. It's what Laura and I have always done. Laura even made the varsity soccer team at Mountain View, but when she and a teammate collided during practice, knocking her out cold, Mom made her quit.

This will be my last year playing soccer and I plan to make the most of it. We start drills and as I complete a wall pass I see these guys as teammates and competition, not potential boyfriends. Even though I think more about boys than sports these days, out here it's different. I can flirt with boys, but also steal the ball from them and score a goal. This is the person Mom, Dad, Chet, Laura, and Mitch all know. This is the Nori they cheer for.

I make a run toward the goal, but the cross sails over my head. I jog back to my position and for the rest of practice I lose myself in tackles and one-touch passes. I'm the same girl I've always been, sprinting across the soccer field; always keeping up.

Couples

One morning, when the chill of fall brings frost to the ground, I'm sitting in Mrs. Whitworth's class reading a poem about "Two roads diverged in a yellow wood." She talks about choices and how one decision can change the rest of your life and you'll never have the chance to go back again.

It reminds me of sixth grade when I liked Duffy and seventh grade when I liked Shawn but kissed Travis, Cougar, and John. Now I'm in eighth grade and all of that feels so distant. Shawn is in high school and it doesn't matter that I liked him for all those months. I glance around the classroom and think maybe I like DJ Brown or Mike Bjorvik, but whatever I decide, that will make all the difference.

After class Dayna passes me a note telling me Ezra asked who I like. Even though we hang out in the same crowd, Ezra and I barely talk. I've always thought he was cute with his bleach-blonde hair and boyish charm. Besides, after Gabe, he's probably the coolest guy in school. I'd be crazy not to go out with him. I write back to Dayna.

DAYN- REALLY? EZRA? SURE, I COULD LIKE HIM. NOR

Later that day Gabe asks me if I want to go with Ezra and I say yes.

Two days later we get out at 12:30. Jamie, Kim, Gabe, Ezra, Chris Rexrode, and I walk over to Ezra's house even though Mom thinks I'm going to Dayna's. It's sunny but not too hot, and I watch our shadows stretch across the sidewalk as we head down Neff Road. I can hardly believe how perfect everything is. We're eighth graders. Jamie's going with Gabe, and I'm going with Ezra. Every time Ezra looks at me warmth spreads throughout my body like it did when I kissed John last spring. At the bottom of the hill Ezra holds my hand and it feels so easy, like we share the same energy as our arms swing together. Jamie and I chat, and I try to hide how anxious I am about what might happen when we get to Ezra's house with no adults around.

Ezra's house is new and the walls are bright white. Jamie and Gabe find a spot on the couch in front of the TV and Chris puts *The Texas Chainsaw Massacre* into the VCR. Ezra and I sit together on the plush white carpet. Kim and Chris disappear upstairs somewhere. Jamie looks so comfortable leaning into Gabe on the couch. She smiles and laughs as Gabe pulls a blanket over the two of them. I have no idea what to say to Ezra. He laces his fingers between mine and even though my eyes are on the TV I have no idea what's going on in the movie. Ezra puts his arm around my shoulder and leans over to kiss me. Ezra has kissed a lot of girls. He's chewing gum so his mouth is sweet and minty. I'm glad I got my braces off last week because as we kiss my bare teeth graze against his and it feels even better than any other kiss I've had before.

Ezra's hand slides down from my shoulder down, stops on my chest. I start breathing harder because I'm letting him get to second base. He slides his hand under my t-shirt and feels over the top of my bra. We're still kissing, his warm fingers rubbing against my bra, when someone thumps down the stairs. He pulls his hand away and we stare at the TV. Kim tells us her mom is going to pick her up. I glance at the VCR clock: 1:45. Jamie and Gabe peek out from underneath a blanket and I catch Jamie's eye. We have to go.

Jamie and I get up to leave as a chainsaw whines from the TV. Gabe walks us to the door. I wave bye to Ezra but he's talking to Chris in the kitchen. Something in me starts to tug, a sinking feeling in my chest that I ignore.

Jamie and I walk against a strong headwind up the hill, giddy to be two best friends going out with the two coolest boys at school. I tell Jamie I think I really like Ezra. She doesn't have to say a thing. I know exactly how she feels about Gabe.

When I get home, Mom asks about my day and I shrug. The less I tell her the better. She can never know I didn't go to

Dayna's and instead I made out with a boy and watched a rated R movie. I can barely look at her or she'll catch me, so I head up to my room.

I turn on the radio and wonder what Ezra is doing. Is he going to call me? I feel that tug again. Maybe I should call him. I decide not to. I can be aggressive with boys on the soccer field, but not with my boyfriend.

Ezra and I barely talk for the rest of the week and a sinking feeling in my chest replaces the excitement I felt before. On Friday, Ezra breaks up with me. I try to figure out what I did wrong. I think through every choice I made. Maybe I should have called, or tried to talk to him during lunch, or after volleyball practice. I wonder if any of these choices would have made a difference. Then I remember the Robert Frost poem about two roads and how "I doubted if I should ever come back." I'll never know why we broke up, and I'm glad I didn't let him feel under my bra.

Chemical Energy

Jamie's mom drives east of town, away from the river and toward Kim's house. Last year Kim didn't invite us to her birthday party, but this year she invites everyone. Maybe we've learned from what happened with Robin that our group doesn't need to be so exclusive. Kim invites Bianca, Jamie, Dayna, and even Val who we worked so hard to exclude last year. Tara Farsvedt, Darci Fassett and the new girl, Jen Clark, are there too. We show up at Kim's house for a scavenger hunt, presents, cake, and ice cream and everyone gets along just fine. When Mom picks Jamie and me up to take us home we're still electric from the energy of the party.

In science we're studying the periodic table, how electrons spin around the nucleus and elements bond together. All matter interacts this way, so it seems like all the eighth graders should be able to hang out together. Who knows what kinds of interactions and bonds we might create.

We plan to go to the movies on Friday night and I tell Bianca, "We should invite everyone." Bianca nods. She probably thinks everyone equals our usual friends so I add, "How cool would it be if like 50 people showed up."

Bink recalculates what I mean by everyone and says, "Yeah, that would be cool," and I know she gets it because when we see Sarah Hogan walking ahead of us she shouts for her to wait and invites her to the movies on Friday.

The invitation spreads quickly. Everyone from Kim's birthday is going, and Gabe and all his friends, along with just about any eighth grader who talks to any of us: Chad Davidson and Joe Speck, DJ Brown and Isaac Howe, Tara Transue and Tara Duncan, Melissa Jacobson and Linnea Ferrin.

We all meet at The Tower downtown for *La Bamba* and sort ourselves into seats next to friends or potential boyfriends. Each of us is an atom with electrons buzzing around a nucleus and in those first few moments we move and trade seats, create and break bonds until our manic energy sinks deep into the dark seats of the theatre. Couples move to the back and the rest of us sneak peaks over our shoulders to catch our friends trading sloppy kisses in the glow of the screen. I barely notice the movie until Ritchie Valens' plane crashes and the bonds with his mom, his brother, and his girlfriend are all broken.

The credits roll and we walk into the bright light of the lobby. We break bounds and reform groups, electrons still buzzing, highly attuned to finding out what happened in the dark of the theatre. Whispers pass from one group to another about hands disappearing under shirts and bras. Electrons dance as we hear about the boy who unsnapped her jeans and the girl who let his fingers explore her.

Cars pull up and the energy of the group disintegrates into the night. We wave bye before disappearing into cars where our chemical properties shift to match the innocent kids we are with our families.

Dad pulls up in the Honda and my body still buzzes from the chemical energy of the night. I watch the headlights of the car lead us home.

Dad grips the steering wheel. "So, how was the movie?"

I slow my electrons from spinning and recall the movie's plot. The images from the movie match pictures of Dad when he was a teenager with slicked-back hair and jeans rolled up. I hadn't noticed, but the movie had things in common with Dad's life. "It was good, Dad. You would like it. It's about Ritchie Valens."

"Oh, okay," Dad answers, but he doesn't believe me. Maybe he can tell I didn't really watch the movie and I'm still thinking about what happened in the dark of the theatre. Maybe he can tell I feel bad because I didn't even think about everything he had in common with the movie until he asked about it. We don't talk for the rest of the drive and in the silence the energy from my night fades away.

Halloween

During choir on the Wednesday before Halloween Gabe tells me he's going to break up with Jamie.

"Really?" I ask. I'm worried. Jamie really likes Gabe and if they break up she'd be crushed. "Why? What's going on?"

"I dunno, it just seems like it's getting too serious."

"Just wait until after Halloween," I tell him.

"Why?"

"Just wait."

Mr. Miller plays a couple of chords on the piano cueing us to warm-up. We breathe and sing scales and Gabe and I don't talk about it again.

All week Jamie's been talking about her Jeanie costume. She hopes when Gabe sees her in it the awkwardness she's noticed between them will go away. Jamie can probably feel that same tug I felt when Ezra was about to break up with me. I hope she can do something to make Gabe change his mind.

On Halloween I wear a witch's hat and all black. Jamie comes to my house in her Jeanie costume and I know she must be freezing in that shiny see-through pink and purple outfit. Kim comes too and she's a pretty princess. I can't figure out when Halloween changed. Instead of being funny or scary, girls' costumes became about what the boys want to see. I don't care though. Mom would never let me wear a sexy costume and there's nothing cute about my witch costume.

Mom takes pictures before we head out into the dark. We skip Robin's house but trick-or-treat all the way to Bianca's. She comes out in a clown costume and I'm glad Bianca chose something funny. We head toward Shepard Road. It's great for trick-or-treating because the houses are close together and you get tons of candy. We make our way through the dark searching the night for the boys. We look for the masks Ezra and Jason wore to school and the football uniform Gabe had on, but we never find them.

We walk back to my house for a sleepover and by the time we get there Jamie's freezing. She borrows a sweatshirt from Bink and we spread our candy across the living room floor. I trade lollipops for chocolate while Jamie tries to hide how disappointed she is Gabe never saw her costume.

Gabe breaks up with Jamie and I wonder if she's going through every move trying to figure out what could have made a difference. I'd hoped Halloween would change things, but it didn't.

"Just forget about him, Jaym," I tell her on the phone but I don't mention how I knew Gabe was going to break up a long time ago. Jamie doesn't say anything. I tell her what I learned from Ezra. "You can't go back and change things," but she doesn't hear me. She wants to try to win him back, but I know Gabe doesn't like her anymore. Simple as that. "I don't think you can do anything, Jaym. Sometimes people just change." I can feel her glaring at me through the silence on the line. "He's just a guy. It's nothing personal."

No matter what I say, though, Jamie's stuck on Halloween. She insists that if Gabe had seen her in her Jeanie costume they would still be together.

Football Games

The first football game of the year is at Bend High. Everyone's going so even though I'm a Mountain View Cougar, I have to be there or I could miss something. Friday after school I have three hours to get ready before Kim's mom picks me up.

I close the door to the bathroom downstairs. I want to try some of Mom's make-up even though I'm not sure how it should look. I stand on my tiptoes to see into the mirror and apply eye shadow, blush, and mascara. I blink at myself in the mirror, unsure if it looks any good. All I know is I definitely look older. Then, I sneak into Laura's room and borrow her white sweater. I stare into the full-length mirror in Mom and Dad's room and hardly recognize my reflection. My dark hair frames a face bright with blush and eyes wide with mascara and eyeliner. The white sweater layers over my jeans and penny loafers perfectly.

Kim's mom honks outside.

I have to get out of the house without anyone seeing me. I sprint through the living room, yell bye, and slam the door behind me.

At the football game we hang out in the trees above the south end zone with kids from Cascade. I spot some of last years' eighth graders in the student section with the rest of the high school students. Nothing really happens all night though.

When I get home I try to rush past Laura who's watching TV in the living room.

"Hey, is that my sweater?" She asks and I freeze as she glares at me.

"Yeah, sorry," I say hoping she doesn't ban me from her closet.

"Just ask, Nori." She stares at me. "Are you wearing make-up?" She starts to laugh.

"Yeah, so." I say matching her attitude.

"Well, you look hilarious," she says and then she turns back to the TV. "And don't get any make-up on my sweater," she adds as I stomp upstairs and into the bathroom.

I run the faucet and wait for the water to warm up. My face is flush. I keep hearing Laura's words, "You look hilarious." I glare at the girl staring back at me, ashamed of who I tried to be tonight. Tonight I was a girl who takes her sister's stuff, sneaks into her mother's make-up, and then doesn't even have any fun when she goes out. I splash lukewarm water on my face and watch the colors trail down the drain. Blush, eye shadow, and mascara wash away, and I wish I could figure out who I am.

A week later I ride with Laura to Mountain View for another football game. She let me borrow her grey wool sweater and I'm not wearing any make-up tonight. We don't talk on the drive but I hope Laura sees that I'm not the girl she hated last Friday night.

At the game, Laura sits in the students' section while I sit in the end zone with all the Pilot Butte eighth graders. The boys want to study the game so they'll be ready next year when they go out for football.

Dayna and Gabe sit together because they just started going out, but the rest of us are just friends so we sit under blankets and it's one of those good times.

The new girl, Jen Clark, is there and she and Kim have hit it off so they sit together. Bianca, Jamie, and I share a blanket on the other side of them. Bink and I try to keep Jamie as far away from Gabe and Dayna as we can. Jamie hates Dayna, but I can't blame Dayna for going out with Gabe. Last year she was the new girl and now she's going out with the most popular boy in school. Casey Black, Chris Rexrode, Dally Taylor, Jason Davis, Joe Speck, and Cody French are there too. Casey sits behind me. I've never really talked to him, but he's pretty funny. He isn't really into the game like the other guys and as the cold of night sinks in, he lets me lean back against him. He gradually drapes his arms around me, and even though we aren't going out I feel warm and safe.

Jamie, Bianca, and I go to the bathroom at half time. They ask what's going on with Casey and me.

"I don't know," I shrug. I kind of like him, but I don't know for sure. Bianca went out with him in seventh grade and so did Dayna, but I don't know how cool he is.

"I bet he's going to ask you out," Jamie says. "That would be cool."

"Yeah," says Bianca. "You guys make a cute couple."

That's all the approval I need.

Casey asks me out in the third quarter, and I say yes. I lean back even deeper into him and he nuzzles his face in my neck. Right before the end of the game I turn to check the score so I can tell Mom when she asks and Casey is right there. We kiss and it's the most natural thing, warm, soft, and sugary. I'm not cold anymore and I think back to Travis, John, and Ezra and wonder why kissing them never made me feel like this.

When I climb into the car with Laura I wonder if she can see how flush my face is or tell how much has changed in these few hours. I feel different now that I'm going out with Casey, but I probably look exactly the same on the outside. Laura doesn't say anything and when I get home Mom and Dad are watching TV. I sit on the couch and watch a MASH rerun, but I'm thinking about Casey's arms keeping me warm.

"How was the game?" Mom asks during a commercial.

"It was fun," I say and I hide my smile so my family will still see the same little girl I've always been. They see the old me, but I'm remembering the feeling of Casey's soft brown hair nuzzled against my neck. I want to hold onto the excitement of the night and then the phone rings. I sprint to get it. It's Casey.

"Hi, Nor," he says and his voice is low and quiet like he's sneaking on the phone.

"Hey," I say and I can feel my face getting warm all over again.

"I had a great time tonight," he says.

"So did I," I say through my smile. I hope Mom and Dad aren't listening from the other room.

"I'll call you tomorrow," Casey adds. "Good night."

"Night," I say, and I hang up the phone. I walk past my parents in the living room and head upstairs past the closed doors of Laura and Mitch's rooms. As I climb into bed I feel the girl I am at home drifting further and further away from the girl I am with my friends.

Piano Lessons

When Casey and I talk on the phone it's easy. He hangs out with me most of the time but when he hangs out with the guys, it's not a big deal. We are solid, the perfect couple. I ask him to the Sadie Hawkins dance and that night I wear a soft blue and white flannel and my brand new Guess jeans. It's the first time I've had Guess jeans or a boyfriend for a dance. We dance together for all the slow songs and when he holds me close during "Take My Breath Away" we fit together perfectly. Sometimes we make-out right there on the dance floor.

When we've been going out for a few weeks he comes to the house in the morning and walks me to school. We hold hands the whole way and I don't miss walking with Robin and Bianca at all. We kiss before he goes to band and I go to leadership. For the first time it isn't about my friends or hanging out in a group. It's about Casey and me, alone. He knows how to do everything and I could kiss him forever, even with his braces.

On the Wednesday before Thanksgiving we get out early and Casey comes over after school. The house is cold and empty with Dad at work, Laura at basketball practice, Mitch at wrestling, and Mom at her class at the community college. I'm breaking the no-friends-in-the-house rule but I don't care.

I pull Casey by the hand to the couch and we start kiss. He leans me into the corner of the couch and his weight rests on top of me. I feel something hard pressing against my leg as he reaches under my shirt and unhooks my bra. Every cell in me tingles as he kisses my neck and then cups his hand under my bra. Second base. We kiss and I run my hands through his hair. I could make-out with him all afternoon, but I check the clock glowing from the VCR, 4:00.

I re-hook my bra and Casey looks into my eyes. My whole body is hot even in our cold house and when I walk Casey back up to school I stay warm just holding his hand.

At the next football game Casey and I huddle together in the end zone. It's our anniversary. We've been going out for three weeks and we're here at the football field where we first got together. I remember last year when I didn't know why the eighth grade couples went up to the dark of the baseball field. Now, I know, and even though most junior high couples don't last I think Casey and I will be together forever.

The next week Casey comes over after school again. We're messing around on the couch but this time his hands slide along my stomach and he unbuttons my jeans. I reach down and unbutton his. He holds my hips as we rock up and down, pressing against one another, and for the first time I can imagine how great sex must feel. He guides my hand to feel him and presses his fingers into me. We breathe hard into one another's necks, and kiss like we want to consume one another.

The VCR clock glows: 4:00. "You have to go," I tell him as I smile even though I really want him to stay. I arch my back, re-hook my bra, and zip up my jeans. We stand and I smooth my hair and clothes. We walk toward the garage door, but then he pushes me up against the piano. The keys clang into the silence of the empty house. We kiss again, gently at first, then harder, and he presses me into the piano keys. We giggle at the noise, so loud in the hallow house. He pulls my shirt up and I close my eyes as he kisses me. I lean my hands onto the piano and the sound of the keys keeps me from hearing the door opening.

Laura is there in the doorway.

I yank down my shirt and Casey straightens up. The piano sounds awkwardly again as I pull off the keys. Laura rushes past us, past the piano, her piano, the one she's played ever since we were little. She doesn't look at me and I can tell she's disgusted. She pounds up the stairs and Casey laughs. I laugh too, but deep down I want to cry. Even though I love who I am with Casey, I hate the girl Laura just saw.

I walk Casey back up to school and then turn back toward home. The wind picks up so I walk faster and crunch through the leaves. It feels like it might snow tonight. I see our gray house matching the dark sky on Jones Road and wonder if Laura will say anything to Mom.

It's quiet when I walk in the front door. The piano and the couch look different now, like they hold secrets for me. I hear the creak of floorboards upstairs but Laura doesn't come down. What will she think the next time she practices piano? The next time she looks at me? Will she tell Mom and Dad?

I hear the garage door open and Mom pulls into the driveway. I help her make dinner. I'm chopping onions when Laura comes in the kitchen for a glass of milk. She doesn't look at me or mention a thing. She never does.

I hope she's forgotten all about that afternoon, but a couple days later she answers the phone. It's Casey and she hands me the receiver like it's contaminated. She looks at me the same way she did when I borrowed her sweater without asking and tried to wear make-up. Maybe she's jealous because I have a boyfriend and she doesn't, or maybe she thinks I'm a slut. I'm sure she never let a boy touch her the way she saw Casey touch me. I tell myself I don't care if Laura hates me, but I hope she doesn't. After all, I'm still her little sister.

Winter Break

The Mountain View Mall is decorated for the holidays with fake greenery and red ribbon. Jamie and I are figuring out what I should get Casey for Christmas. I've never had a boyfriend during the holidays, and I want to get him the perfect present. I've figured out the formula for friends and popularity, but relationships are complicated. I still can't figure out why Ezra broke up with me, or why Jamie and Gabe didn't work out. I don't know why DJ Brown and I have slow-danced together since the sixth grade but have never gone out or why Dayna broke up with Gabe last week. Relationships are harder to figure out than friendships and I don't want to mess things up with Casey.

Jamie and I walk through the perfume section at the Emporium because cologne seems like the safest choice. Jamie and I found our scents in the seventh grade (she wears Giorgio and I wear Poison). We start with Drakkar Noir, but that smells like Gabe. Then it's Polo, but Shawn wore that and I don't want Casey smelling like my crush from last year. I'm pretty sure Casey wears Chaps, so I should either get him that or something that smells like it. I wish Casey wore something cooler, but Chaps already makes me think of him so I buy him a bottle. It comes wrapped in a brown box with a dark red ribbon. It's perfect.

It snows the day before Christmas vacation and the whole world glitters in the winter light. I get ready for school early and catch a ride with Laura so I don't have to walk in the snow. Today we have a noon dance, but instead of looking forward to the slow songs and dancing with Casey all I want to hear is George Michael's "Faith" or The Bangles' "Walk Like an Egyptian." Casey watches as I dance with the girls and something annoys me about his smile. When they play "Hungry Eyes" from Dirty Dancing I dance with him, but something feels different. Something in the formula of our relationship has changed. By the time the song ends, I know I'm going to break up with him.

After school Casey and I wait for his school bus. I'm not sure when I'll see him again so I hand him his present. He seems to like it, and then he hands me a small box. Jewelry. I hope it's not earrings because I don't have my ears pierced, and it better not be a ring because that would be way too serious. I tear off the Christmas paper and open the white jewelry box. It's a gold necklace with a heart charm.

"It's Black Hills Gold," Casey says as he secures the tiny clasp around my neck.

I wince because this must have cost a lot more that a bottle of Chaps. "Casey, this is too much. You shouldn't have." The chain falls cold against my skin and Casey leans in to kiss me. I don't want to kiss him though so I turn my head and give him a hug. I have to get away. The smell of his cologne is too much. His bus pulls up.

"Thanks, Casey. It's really nice."

"Merry Christmas, Nori." He holds my cheeks in his warm hands. "Love ya."

"You too." I say and I give him a quick kiss before pulling away. I look over my shoulder and start walking away. Usually I wait for his bus to leave, but I want to catch up with Bianca so I walk quickly toward Shepard Road.

Dark clouds have rolled over the mountains making it seem even later than 3:15. It might snow tonight and I hope we'll have a ton of snow for Christmas. I find Bianca walking along the ditch with Jason Davis and Mike Bjorvick. Once we get to her house, I let the boys walk ahead so I can talk to Bink about Casey.

"Look what he gave me." I pull the necklace toward her.

"It's so pretty, Nor. It looks expensive." Bianca studies the necklace in her gloved hand.

I look over my shoulder to make sure the boys are gone. "I know, but I don't think I like him anymore. I want to break up."

"Really?" Bianca lets go of the necklace. "Do you have to give it back if you break up?"

"I don't know." I can't even think about that. I can't get over the annoyed feeling I had today.

"Well, you should wait until after Christmas. Call me later and we'll talk about it."

I walk home over red cinders, snow, and ice and think about how much things can change in a day. I try to remember how I felt the last time Casey and I were alone. I want to remember how great it felt to kiss him so I won't have to break up, but I can only remember feeling annoyed by him at the dance. Bianca's right. I should wait, but I don't want to pretend things are okay. I want to get it over with. I drag the gold heart along the thin chain. It's warm in my fingers from being next to my skin. I wish I still liked him. If I did this necklace would feel amazing.

Coming up Jones Road the bounce of a basketball echoes through the quiet. I hear voices. Joe, Chad, and DJ are playing basketball with Mitch in the backyard. I drop my backpack in the garage and shoot around with the guys. The ball feels comfortable in my hand and as I pull ahead in our game of 21, I forget about Casey. I don't call Bianca or Jamie to talk about it. I feel light and carefree. I am the Nori who plays with the guys, who doesn't care about boys, whose sister would be proud of her for making all her free throws. I can be this girl again.

We turn on the outdoor lights and tiny snowflakes drift out of the darkness. Every so often, I feel the tickle of the necklace on my neck and it makes my heart sink.

When the phone rings inside, I know it's going to be him. I run inside and it's too hot in the kitchen. I pick up the phone and drag the heart along the gold chain. "Hi, Casey. I can't really talk. I'm kinda busy." I look out at the boys playing in the backyard, and I want to be free.

"What're you doing?"

"Oh, you know, just family stuff. I'll call you tomorrow." I want to break up with him, but I think about what Bianca said and feel the weight of the necklace against my neck. I hang up the phone and take the necklace off. I think I might cry. My heart pounds against my chest. I'm not sure if it's because I've been playing basketball or because of what I'm about to do. I don't think about it. It just feels right. I dial his number, and Casey picks up on the first ring. "I'm sorry, Casey, but I think we should break up." Almost as soon as the words fall out, I want to take them back. "Do you want your necklace back?" He doesn't say anything, but I can hear him breathing. "Hello?"

"No, I don't want it back," he says. "I got it for you." His voice cracks a little and I wonder if he's crying. I don't know what to say. It's so quiet on the line. Both of us breathe in the awkward silence until he asks, "Did I do something? What happened? Is there someone else?"

"No, no, no," I say as I watch DJ miss a free throw. Chad grabs the rebound, and it's like I'm in a trance. "I just don't want to be with anyone right now. I'm sorry."

"Whatever," he says and hangs up.

I stand in the kitchen as snowflakes float through the dark. I set the phone in its cradle. I think about calling him again, but what would I say?

I head back out into the cold to play basketball. I hit a jumper and I'm the old Nori again. I smile and flirt without a single tinge of guilt, without the cold weight of Casey's necklace bouncing against my chest.

Merry Christmas

I'm eating waffles in the breakfast room, watching the snowfall. The radio just gave the ski report and we should have a great day on the mountain. Laura comes into the breakfast room. I wish I could tell her that Casey and I broke up. Maybe then she'd rethink the kind of girl I am. The phone rings and Mom picks up. It's Jamie.

"Not Casey?" Laura asks with a sneer.

"No," I say as I finish the last of my waffle. "We broke up." I want to see her reaction but instead I head upstairs to take the call. As soon as I hear the click of Mom hanging up the phone downstairs I tell Jamie I broke up and even though she's surprised, I don't want to talk about it. I tell her I have to go. I hang up and get ready to go skiing.

With Chet home the family feels whole again. Dad drives through town and across the Deschutes River with its frozen edges. We wind up Century Drive and I leave my worries about school, boys, and friends behind. I sit between Laura and Mitch like I have for so many years. We are quiet and even though I'm pretty sure they hate me, I hope this week they'll see I'm still the same girl, the same Nori who skis with her family every Christmas. The mountain appears around a corner, and as I stare up at it's enormous glittering slopes, I remember how easy it is to be that girl.

We ski, eat sandwiches in the lodge for lunch, and Dad buys us cocoa and cake donuts like Auntie Grace used to. On Christmas Eve we go to mass and then head over to Eddie's Canton for dinner. It was too quiet last year so this year Mom invites the Curries. They meet us at the restaurant and their three boys wear matching little red bow ties. Their bright eyes and baby-toothed grins remind me how magical Christmas used to be, when baby Jesus, Santa, and flying reindeer were all real.

For Christmas my family gets me the coolest gifts: the new George Michael tape, a stonewashed Guess Jean jacket, a Coca-Cola sweatshirt and an INXS KICK shirt. Maybe they do know the girl I am at school and maybe they don't hate me after all. I'm glad I don't have to worry about Casey calling and reminding Laura of our secret, or Chet and Mitch teasing me about my little boyfriend. I don't have to ignore the looks Mom and Dad give one another whenever a boy calls. I can just be Nori: the littlest Nakada who helps Mom in the kitchen and watches football.

Christmas night winds down and even though I feel bad about breaking up with Casey, it's exactly what I needed to fold back into the world of my family. Being together, all six of us, reminds me that even though Chet has left for college and Laura will do the same next year, even though I'm trying to figure out who I am away from this family, I will always be a Nakada.

Ringing in a New Year

A couple of days after Christmas I go over to Jen Clark's house. She's new this year and at first I didn't like her. She seemed stuck up and she liked Casey when we first started going out. But Casey and I aren't together anymore, so when she invites me over I figure we might as well be friends.

Her house reminds me of Aunt Bev's. It smells like cigarettes and animals. We baby-sit for her neighbor for a couple hours and when we go to change the little boy's diaper we examine his little penis and laugh about how ugly and wrinkly it is. While the baby naps, we listen to George Michael, and put on make-up. We're sitting on the floor in her bedroom in front of a big mirror leaned against the wall. Jen looks at my reflection.

"Hey, Nori, is it okay if I call Casey?"

"I thought you liked Ezra."

"Well, I did. But, you know, I always thought Casey was cute. I won't call him if you don't want me to. It's just, I thought *you* broke up with *him*."

"Yeah, I did." I watch Jen's fiddling with a compact of pressed powder. I imagine how hard it must be to start at a new school in the eighth grade. "Sure, do whatever you want."

Jen smiles. I know she's right. I did break up with him so it should be okay, but I'm burning inside. I hang out a little longer, but then I call Mom to pick me up.

Jamie calls the next day to tell me Jen and Casey are going out.

"Whatever," I say. "I don't like him anymore anyway." I twist the phone cord around my finger. My fingertip turns red and fat. My pulse throbs at the end of my finger as Jamie tells me all about her Christmas gifts. I don't tell her I think I made a mistake: that I never should have broken up with Casey.

I convince Mom to let me go to Jason Davis's New Year's Eve party. It's freezing and the roads are icy as I walk to his house alone. Instead of loving my new freedom, I feel lonely. I wish I had someone to kiss this New Year, but Casey is going to be with Jen at this party.

Dayna, Jason, Mike, and I play with the Ouija board in Jason's bedroom. I can tell Dayna's moving it even though she swears she isn't. Jason likes Dayna but she doesn't like anyone. By 10:30 I'm sick of the party. I've eaten too many Cool Ranch Doritos and it's a lot of work avoiding the living room where Jen and Casey and the rest of the couples are making out. I think about walking home early, ringing in the New Year with my family, eating sushi and tempura, and banging pots at midnight. But it's cold outside, and I don't want to be alone. I know I'm being a downer. I remember protecting Jamie from Gabe and Dayna when she and Gabe first broke up. I wanted her to get over it, but now I know how she felt. What makes it worse is that I ruined it. I broke up with him. What if I told him I made a mistake? Maybe he'd break up with Jen and we'd get back together.

At midnight we go into the living room to watch the apple drop in Times Square. I hug Dayna and Jamie and pretend I don't see Casey and Jen kissing in the corner. Just after midnight, I head out into the cold, dark night. Stars peek through clearing clouds, but I hardly notice as I tread home.

The lights in our house and in Robin's house are still on. I silently wish Robin a happy New Year and head through the front door. Mitch and Laura watch music videos in the living room. Earlier I thought they were lame for staying home on New Year's Eve, but now I think they had it right. They don't say anything to me. No happy New Year. Nothing. I wonder what's happened since Christmas when I felt like I was part of the family. Now I feel separate all over again.

Mom's cleaning up the kitchen. "You're home early."

"Yeah," I say opening a box of Ritz crackers. "I should have just stayed home."

"Really? It was your first New Year's party."

"It wasn't as great as I thought it would be." I look down, not wanting Mom to see how hurt I am. I don't want her to ask because I couldn't talk to her about it anyway.

Mom dries her hands on a towel and gives me a little squeeze. "Well, happy New Year, Nori."

I don't hug her back or I'll start to cry. "Thanks, Mom. Happy New Year to you too." I head upstairs to my cold room unsure how I've managed to become so miserable with both my friends and my family.

Instincts

After winter break, even though Casey is still going out with Jen, when Bianca, Kim, or Jamie asks who I like I tell them I still like Casey. Jen ignores me so I figure word has gotten around. I never tell Casey I like him so it's not like I'm trying to break them up. I know Casey will find out though, and I hope he'll choose me. After all, we had something special. We went out for almost three months and I still wear the necklace he gave me for Christmas as proof. He and Jen have only been going out for a week. She's totally his rebound.

On Wednesday Kim passes me a note between third and fourth period. She has on a big, silly smile, so I know it must be something good. I unfold the notebook paper in science.

Nori (the V.P.)!

What are you doing? Duh, reading this. Ha, okay, so... do you still like C.B. 'cause I talked to him today and he thinks he still likes you! Crazy! He said he's breaking up after school. Oh my gosh. W.B. if you like him for sure.

Kim

I don't think of Jen at all. I just think about how good Casey made me feel and how depressed I've been since New Year. I'm so excited and when I pass him in the hall between fifth and sixth, the passing period when he used to meet me at my locker and walk me to class, I catch his eye and smile.

Casey calls me after school and asks me out. He makes me feel a little bad about before and I tell him I'm sorry; I was stupid. I didn't know what I wanted. He has to go and even though I want it to feel like it did before, something's different. Kim calls me to tell me Casey and Jen broke up and I tell her he already asked me out.

"Jen's going to be so mad," Kim says.

"She must have known this might happen. She was just his rebound."

I can't wait to be alone with Casey again. I imagine kissing him and how perfect it will be, but all week there's no chance for us to hang out. On Friday night everyone makes plans to go to the Bend High boys' basketball game, but I'm going to watch my sister at Mountain View. I could miss out on a big night, but for the past year-and-a-half I've put friends first and family second. Tonight I'm trying to strike a balance. Besides, it's Laura's senior year and she's going away to college in a few months. She's my sister. She still sobs at night, and she never told anyone about that afternoon at the piano. Besides, basketball might be the only thing Laura and I still have in common. Tonight I choose family.

I walk through the empty second floor of the gym as the second half starts. Laura dribbles up the court and hits a pull-up jumper. I cheer and know I've made the right decision. It's the road less taken, and even though I doubt I should ever come back, it's where I'm supposed to be.

As the game clock ticks down a knot grows inside me. If I've done the right thing, why are my instincts telling me something is wrong? I can't figure it out. Mountain View wins, and Laura scores 24 points, but my stomach is knotted so tight I can't take a full, deep breath.

It's almost ten o'clock when I get home. I call Casey, but his sister answers and says he's at a friend's house all weekend.

For two long days the phone doesn't ring. Casey never calls. Neither do Jamie, Kim, Bianca, or Dayna. My heart feels heavy. My stomach churns in a way I've never felt before. Something is wrong. I want to scream but don't know why.

I call Jamie, tell her I feel weird, and ask her about Friday night. She tells me she's sure everything will be okay, but she has to go. She doesn't want to talk to me either. That night I can hardly fall asleep. My mind spins in the silence.

Monday morning at school people say hi and wave, but no one will make eye contact. I've missed something and no matter how I add things up I can't figure out what it might be. I see Dayna before third period and she gives me a hug. "What's going on?" I ask her. "Everyone's acting totally weird."

"I'll tell you later." Dayna can't look me in the eye either, but I grab her by the arm before she turns away. She finally looks at me. "I'll tell you later, Nori. I promise."

I try to pretend everything is okay. During choir I watch everyone like I'm invisible. Bianca talks with Val by the door. Gabe and Cody debate a football game. Dayna comes in with some excuse she used to get out of yearbook. I ask Mr. Miller if I can go to the restroom and meet Dayna outside the choir room. It's quiet and cold even with the sun reflecting off the building. "I'm sorry I didn't tell you sooner," Dayna says as we walk to C Hall. "Casey cheated on you Friday night with Jen."

The energy that had been churning in my stomach and catching in my throat explodes. I almost scream. My face grows hot and I imagine Casey and Jen together, kissing and laughing just like on New Year's Eve. I clench my fists tight. I want to hit something.

"I knew it," I say and I think I might throw up. I step toward the bathroom. "I knew something was wrong. Why didn't anyone tell me?" I feel like such a fool, being oblivious all this time.

Dayna doesn't say anything.

"I'm breaking up."

"No, Nori, you should talk to him."

"No way." I try to breathe but the lump in my throat is about to erupt into tears. I will not cry over a stupid boy and he will never see he's hurt me. "I'm never talking to him again. Will you go tell him? I can't be with him for one more second."

Dayna nods and goes to find Casey.

I slide down the hallway wall to the floor outside Mrs. Whitworth's room. All through middle school I've been hearing about choices, changes, and coming of age: boys' voices change, girls start their periods. We fight for independence from our families, choose friends, boyfriends, and girlfriends.

My mistake was choosing Casey. He stole my innocence and now it's shattered; scattered into pieces across the shiny hallway floor. Dayna comes back and tells me it's done. "I have to get back to class." She looks down at me. "You okay?"

I nod and look up at her. She was the only one brave enough to tell me, of all my friends. "Thanks, Dayn."

She gives my shoulder a squeeze and heads back to class. I can't stand up yet. I hear Mrs. Whitworth talking about Anne Frank and the holocaust. We've been looking at black and white photographs; learning about the inhumane ways people treat one another. I'm learning first hand how awful people can be. Friends, people you know and care about, people who are supposed to love you, hurt you. Mom has told me again and again: life isn't fair. Now I feel it. I know it's true.

I take a deep breath and then another. My heartbeat slows. I'm better than Casey. I never should have gone out with him again. I curse my miscalculation and then catch my breath. I dry my cheeks in the empty hall, breathe, and tell myself I will be okay. I head back to class and clear my face of any emotion. Even though everything has changed, I don't let it show.

During English, Kim and Bianca ask Mrs. Whitworth if they can talk to me. She lets us use a little office cluttered with piles of papers and empty coffee cups. I lean against the counter and a couple of tears escape.

"We're so sorry, Nor."

"We just didn't know what to say."

I tell them I don't care.

"You were too good for him anyway."

"Jen's a total bitch."

"I don't care," I say and my voice sounds strange.

They tell me there are other fish in the sea and I could go out with some many other boys. I nod, but I don't care. I tell them I don't care so many times I start to believe it. I breathe and blink until the air flows and there are no more tears. The bell rings and the hall fills with the noise. Bianca and Kim give me a hug and I tell them, "Whatever, life goes on."

By basketball practice I've forgiven my friends who didn't tell me. I escape into lay-ups, jump-shots and a smothering defense that gives me five steals. I wonder if that's why Laura's so good at basketball. Maybe she takes all of her late-night tears and pours them out on the court.

I walk home alone, talk briefly with Jamie on the phone, ignore my siblings, and watch *The Wonder Years*. The next day the sun comes up and I walk to school. I go to class and pass notes. I complete my work and pretend to pay attention. But the way the sunlight filters through the trees, the way stars litter the night sky, the way icicles hang from the rooftops; it all looks different. I watch my friends and family like an outsider. I look for signs of lying. I wonder what Mitch and Laura are going through and what they're thinking about, but I never ask. They don't ask about my life either, and even if they did, I couldn't explain how my view of the world has shifted. We continue to walk around one another in the quiet of home.

The thing is, I can't believe no one notices. No one sees I've gone quiet. Not Jamie, Bianca, Dayna, or Kim. Not Mom or Dad, Mitch or Laura. The people I thought knew me best don't care that a light that once glowed within me has been snuffed out. I study myself in the bathroom mirror, look for the joy that used to shine from my eyes, and even I can't see it. I look exactly the same, but I feel completely different. I look out my bedroom window. The sky is dark, starless. The lights at Robin's house are out. The world has gone dark. I wish I could change it. I wish I could go back, but this is who I am now.

Rebound

Thank God it's basketball season. Even though I struggle through the Casey break up and adjust to my new dark perspective on life, I have a clear plan for the future. Laura is going to play college ball next year and someday I will too. I have to focus, work harder at basketball than anyone in our small town, harder than anyone in Portland or Los Angeles, and make it out of here.

Every night after school and practice, between talking on the phone and avoiding homework, I head out to the backyard to shoot around. I imagine leading my team to the Final Four and a TV crew coming to Bend, to this backyard where Nori Nakada grew up, where she used to shovel snow in order to practice free throws, lay-ups, and three-point shots. I count down the seconds on an imaginary clock. I dribble, change directions, jump-stop, shoot, and score.

We win the first couple games of the season, but our next game is at Madras. On the bus ride we cross the Crooked River Gorge and I think about the girls from the Warm Spring Indian Reservation who go to the school in Madras. Those are the girls I have to worry about. There's nothing else for kids on the Rez to do but play ball, so the point guards are quick and can dribble left or right. The forwards and centers know how to post up and always make their lay-ups. Girls from the Rez are tough. They play fast and physical.

The Madras team wears mustard yellow uniforms. They don't have anyone as tall as Candice, our center, but there are three Native girls. My dark straight hair matches theirs, and I wonder if people think I'm Native American too. Dad says the Forest Service hired him thinking he was from the Rez, but Dad's full Japanese and I'm only half. Maybe they think I'm half Warm Spring Indian, or maybe they just see me as another white-girl from Bend. I doubt they can tell I'm half Asian. People can rarely tell just from looking. I just hope they don't think I'm a sell-out who left the Rez and is trying to fit in with the rich Bend kids.

We win the tip and even though we're taller, the Madras team is deeper. Dayna, Candice, and I match up well, but at the other positions the Madras girls run circles around us. Candice keeps us in the game with a few big rebounds, but I struggle to get around my defender. She's quick and never seems to tire. My defense keeps her from scoring, but we still find ourselves down eight at the half. We fight back in the second half, and I finally make a couple shots from outside. I get fouled on an inbounds play and hit both free throws, but in the fourth quarter we're down four. As the clock winds down, even though I fight for position under the hoop and put back an offensive rebound at the buzzer, it's not enough to win.

The bus ride home is quiet. I don't want to admit we lost. I'd been telling everyone we were going to go undefeated. The bus crosses the high desert as the sun falls behind the snow-covered Cascades. Junipers press black branches against the darkening sky and patches of old snow become a blur as we speed back to Bend. We cross the Crooked River Gorge again and I don't look down. Instead I think about our next big game against Cascade. Lori Bohnenkamp is on that team and if we're going to win, I have to play better.

When I get home, I don't say anything when Mom asks about the game. Instead I turn on the lights in the backyard, and head outside to shoot. I stop trying to calculate where I went wrong with Casey and start figuring out how to win games.

When the boys team plays Madras, I ask Coach Smith if I can ride to the game and keep stats. He agrees, so Dayna and I go to Madras for the second time in a week. During warm-ups and the first quarter I study the game. I search between the lines of the court for a solution that will help me win a ticket away from this small town life. In sixth grade I calculated the formula for popularity. In seventh grade I figured out how to stay popular and cultivate kisses. Now, in eighth grade, I want something bigger. I want something beyond the mountains towns and Indian Reservations of Central Oregon.

Robert is the point guard for the boys. I watch his long, lanky, slightly pigeon-toed style, and he reminds me of Michael Jordan. Robert and I have been friends since sixth grade math class. He's half-Polynesian and I wonder if anyone thinks he's from the Rez. Robert is the best player on the court. He dribbles effortlessly through his legs and behind his back. He pushes the tempo, hits a couple of outside shots, and I slowly develop a crush. I've never liked Robert, but it doesn't matter anyway. He has a girlfriend.

At half-time I ask Dayna what she thinks about Robert and she knows why I'm asking. "He and Jackie have been going out since volleyball season," she says.

I shrug.

"You guys would be a cute couple though."

I wonder if she's only saying that because we're both half-Asian. I've never gone out with someone like me before.

"I don't think they'll ever break up," she adds.

"Yeah," I say as I watch Robert steal the ball and make a lay-up. "People used to say that about Casey and me."

Without noticing, my focus shifts from figuring out how to escape Bend through basketball, to how to get Robert to see me not as a friend, or a good basketball player. I want him to see me in as a girlfriend.

Robert is in my Algebra class and since we've been friends for so long no one thinks it's weird when I move to work with him, DJ, and Isaac. Mandy, Jackie's best friend, sits on the other side of the room and sees me talking with Robert every day. I don't tell anyone how I feel about Robert. We solve inequalities, talk about basketball, and I work carefully. One miscalculation could turn my positive friendship with Robert negative.

Just before the bell, I pack up my stuff and Val leans over. "Hey, Nor, do you like Robert?"

I suppress a smile and then shake my head. "No," I tell her. "He's with Jackie, and they are a sweet couple." I won't be that girl, the girl Jen was with Casey and me.

The next day in Algebra when we finish our homework, I ask Robert how things are with Jackie. He shrugs and says things are fine.

"Cool," I say. He doesn't see me as anything but a friend, but someday, when there is trouble, I'll be there, waiting for the rebound.

Truth or Dare

Kim, Bianca, Jamie, and I are at Dayna's house for a slumber party. We dance around her living room to George Michael and then lay out our sleeping bags. It's time for truth or dare. I don't know why we always play this game. No one wins and there's always the risk of losing. Dares embarrass and truths cut too close the quick. There is pressure not only to respond wisely, but to come up with a truth or dare that will bring us closer, make us squirm, or laugh, or learn something about one another we don't already know.

I want to go first. I know it takes a while for the game to warm up. No one will dare you to poop in a pot and cook it or call Cougar and tell him you're in love with him until at least the second round.

"Truth or dare," Dayna asks me.

"Truth." I can handle truths better than dares that involve getting naked or making prank calls.

"Okay, if you could get back together with any of your ex-boyfriends again, who would it be?"

I run through memories of Jimmy Olsen in fifth grade, Duffy in sixth grade, Travis, Cougar, and John in seventh grade, Ezra, and Casey this year and I know my answer. "I don't want to be with any of those guys again." I pause for effect. "That's the truth."

A groan rises from the group.

"Okay, but what if you *had* to kiss one of them again," Dayna pushes.

I never kissed Jimmy or Duffy, definitely not Travis. "Fine, Ezra," I say but I'm not really sure it's true. If I could go back to when things were right with Casey, before I broke up with him, before he and Jen went out, before he cheated on me, I would choose him. But what is done is done, and Ezra is the coolest guy I've ever kissed so I pick him. It's the safest.

"Okay, Dayna," I say, anxious to get the focus off me. "Truth or Dare."

"Dare."

"Call Peter Obie and play 'I Want Your Sex' for him."

She does this (Dayna will do anything) and I doubt Pete, a sophomore at Mountain View, suspects a bunch of middle school girls would prank call him. The anonymity of this dare makes it easy.

"Okay, I've got one," Kim says and she leans into the circle. "Bianca, truth or dare."

"Truth."

"Tell each of us one thing you hate about us."

"Ooh, good one," I say because everyone wants to know what everyone really thinks. "We should all do it," I suggest. Then everyone has to be truthful and everyone has to be the target. This might be a bad idea, though. Sometimes the truth hurts.

"Okay," Bink starts and I know she's smart enough to think of answers that are true but also not so bad. "I hate Dayna because your mom lets you dye your hair and there's no way I could. Jamie, sometimes you wear too much Giorgio."

She's going around the circle and I'm next.

"Nori, I hate how you are better than me at every sport and Kim..."

She pauses a minute. I think about all of the things Bianca has said when she's been annoyed with Kim.

"I hate how fake you are sometimes."

Ouch. But Kim came up with the dare so Bink must figure she deserves the most honest response.

Now it's Jamie's turn and Bianca has pushed us to the edge of how brutal we can be. Jamie says she hates how Bianca gets the best clothes whenever she wants them. She hates how Dayna never calls back (but we all know that Jamie really hates Dayna for going out with Gabe again.) Jamie hates how I'm friends with all the boys in our class, but when she gets to Kim she says she hates how Kim has gone further than any of us with a boy. She practically calls her a slut.

Kim sinks inside herself. Should I stop this, or are we pushing Kim to the edge tonight? She starts to cry, and she has to know what we're all thinking. We've been annoyed ever since her bet with Dally Taylor.

Everyone knew Kim liked Dally, but they weren't going out. At basketball practice Kim bet Dally that if he made a half-court shot she'd do something none have us had done before. So, of course, he shot, and missed but then Kim said he could try as many times as he wanted. I rolled my eyes. I knew eventually he'd make it, but Kim insisted he'd never be able to make it. Dally shot again, and again, and again, and eventually that ball arched perfectly through the florescent light of the gym, hung forever in the air, and then fell cleanly through the net. The girls all looked at one another and Kim's mouth hung open. She couldn't believe he actually made it. That shot unleashed a new truth for all of us. The boys no longer thought about French kisses, or sliding a hand under a bra or down a girl's pants. Now they thought about what *we* would be willing to do for *them*.

Tears fall down Kim's cheeks and maybe it's because Kim is class president and her mom is the coolest. Maybe it's because she's brave enough to do things none of us can imagine, but we all nod in agreement. Kim runs to the restroom and Bianca goes to talk to her. Jamie, Dayna, and I stare at one another.

"Was I too mean?"

"No. It's not like you called her a slut."

We crawl into our sleeping bags and Dayna puts on the *Less Than Zero* soundtrack. We listen to "Hazy Shade of Winter" and Kim eventually comes back. She looks okay, but as we drift off to sleep I wonder how much damage we've done.

Secrets

I can't fall asleep. I stare at the ceiling and think through the secrets I hold. Dayna wants to break up with Gabe, but I can't tell anyone. Bianca likes a seventh grader, but she doesn't want anyone to know. I have a crush on Robert, but can't say anything because he's still with Jackie. I can't let anyone know what Laura saw Casey and I doing, or how much I miss a boy holding me, pressing into me. I don't tell anyone how guilty I feel every time I look over at Robin's house knowing it's partly my fault she doesn't go to Pilot Butte anymore.

I toss and turn as deeper secrets rise to the surface. Don't think about Chet's breakdown, or Laura's tears at night, or Mom and Dad in counseling. Then there's the secret I haven't mentioned to anyone.

The night when Casey cheated on me, while I was watching my sister in the Mountain View gym, as Jen and Casey were messing around, I knew something was wrong. Maybe I'm psychic. Maybe I have a gift like the oracles at Delphi. But it's no gift. It's a curse. I couldn't stop that terrible night from happening. I could feel the awful events unfolding, but there was nothing I could do to stop fate.

My mind whirls. I wonder if I made all of this happen, if choosing the road less traveled really made all the difference, or if this is the path fate has chosen for me.

I can't stop thinking so I use my insomnia-fighting trick. I picture myself falling into the center of a black hole that never ends. I fall, into inky darkness and spin away from my star-scattered thoughts. The weight of my secrets and lies lifts.

I fall down, down, down, into a dark, heavy sleep.

Grades

Every night after basketball practice I come home and talk on the phone. I listen to the radio and talk on the phone some more. After dinner I make mix tapes of my favorite songs and talk on the phone. I eat dinner, shoot hoops, watch TV, and Mom lets me stay up as long as I still get up for school on time. I never worry about my grades and still pull As and Bs.

Then the second semester progress report comes out. I have a C in English. Mom freaks out. Chet and Laura never got Cs and even though Mitch has, he's special so he gets away with it. Bianca and Kim's moms ground them all the time and Jamie gets put on punishment, but Mom has never done anything like that to me, until now.

"No more phone, no more hanging out with friends after basketball," she says as she shakes my report card. "You come straight home. You do your homework and that's it until the next report card."

"But that's another 5 weeks," I argue. "How will I survive?"

"You'll survive," Mom says.

"I hate you," I yell and stomp upstairs.

Without the phone or hanging out I'll miss everything, but Mom doesn't care. She doesn't even let me answer the phone. She tells all of my friends I'm grounded from the phone and they can talk to me at school.

Since I can't do anything I finish the make-up work for Mrs. Whitworth. I write a story about a woman having an affair using the register of a checkbook. I finish a 20-page poetry anthology. I organize my binder so when Mrs. Whitworth holds the three-ring spine up no papers fall out.

By the end of the week I'm caught up, but Mom still won't let me talk on the phone. With nothing else to do, I head downstairs to watch TV. I plop down on the couch as far away from Mom's recliner as possible. I might be in the same room with her, but I don't have to like it. Dad reads the paper, and

Mom turns on a PBS documentary. Mitch disappears upstairs as the black and white footage cracks across the screen. Martin Luther King Jr., Stokely Carmichael, Freedom Rides, sit-ins. The speeches from *Eyes on the Prize* raise the hairs on the back of my neck. The chants and songs demanding justice and equality make me want to join them, to do something, but the confines of Bend, Oregon close in around me. I've only known one African American in Bend and his white family adopted him. My only sense of injustice is being grounded from the phone. Where do Native Americans from Warm Springs fit into the Civil Rights movement, or Japanese Americans like Dad, or Korean adoptees like Mitch, or half-Japanese girls me? I wish I could be part of something big, something important, something real, but I can't even imagine what that would look like. This mountain town in the middle of Oregon is too far from *Eyes on the Prize* for me to picture it.

I bring my C in English up to an A. Mom lets me use the phone and I disappear back into my room. I catch up on the gossip I missed. I forget about freedom fighters and struggles for equality. I'm too busy solving the problems of eighth grade, and I've already overcome my biggest injustice: being grounded from the phone.

March Madness

This year the NCAA Basketball Final Four is being held in Seattle and Mom and Dad manage to find tickets to the women's semi-final and championship games. We have an extra so I get to invite Dayna because she's serious about basketball too. Besides, Mitch actually likes Dayna, and Chet and Laura don't hate her like some of my other friends.

We drive up to Seattle in two cars and Chet meets us there with some guys from U of O. One of his friends, Brett, is hilarious, and African-American. This confirms what I hoped: college is going to be so much more interesting than life in Bend.

Inside the Tacoma Dome, I feel so small among the thousands of fans from Auburn, Tennessee, Louisiana Tech, and Long Beach State. I cheer with the crowd even though my voice disappears into the arena. When Louisiana Tech wins, I dream I'll be like Teresa Weatherspoon someday. It's the coolest vacation we've ever taken and for the first time since Christmas, I love my family.

Back at school, I lean back in my chair and doodle on a piece of paper to stay awake. Mr. Hess talks about Eli Whitney and how his cotton gin somehow changed everything. Mr. Hess is my least favorite teacher. A couple of weeks ago he kicked me out of class. He said I had an attitude, but I swear I was just sitting there. He made me sit outside even though it was snowing and I was wearing shorts. When I told Mom she complained to the school, but at home she yelled at me for getting kicked out of class. Now I don't say anything in his class. I just sit and sulk.

My eyelids are heavy. I fight my head falling to the desk. I shift in my seat. I have to stay awake, but I'm so tired. We drove back from the Final Four last night so I only got a few hours of sleep. Besides, I'm not interested in calculating proportions of bales of cotton to slaves on a plantation. I'm trying to figure out how someday I'll be running up and down the court in the Women's National Championship game.

The door squeaks open, and Walker Stewart delivers a summons. Mr. Hess sets the slip on my desk. It's from the vice principal, Mr. Mero. Mr. Hess keeps talking as I head out the door toward the main office.

I've been in Mr. Mero's office for student government business, asking if we could host dances or fundraisers, but today when I knock on the doorjamb he doesn't even look up.

"Have a seat Miss Nakada."

I try to remember if I've done anything I shouldn't have. A couple of weeks ago, when there was a sub, we changed the clock in Mr. Hess's class, but that wouldn't be coming up now. I sink into the brown, fake-leather chair across from his desk. Mr. Mero wants to know what I was doing Saturday night.

"I was out of town."

"And where were all your friends?"

"How should I know? I wasn't here." My body temperature rises with each heartbeat.

"Well, were you drinking?"

"Drinking?" I don't know what he's talking about. I got back late last night and I haven't talked to anyone. Besides, even though we're popular, we don't drink or do drugs. We mess around with boys but we never drink. "No, Mr. Mero."

"I'm going to have to call your parents to confirm this," he says. He stands up, cuing me to leave. "I need you to send me Cougar Caverhill."

Mr. Mero hands me a summons and I walk back into Mr. Hess's room. I hand Mr. Hess the office summons as he drones on about the pre-Civil War Southern economy. He gives the summons to Cougar and as he gets up to leave Gabe glances in my direction. I wish I could read Gabe's mind so I knew what was going on.

By lunch everyone has been called into the office: Dayna, Kim, Jamie, and Bianca for the girls, Gabe, Chris Rexrode, Dally, Jason, Cougar and Cody for the boys. Dayna is in tears and she tells me everything. The boys told their parents they were staying over at Jason's, and Jason said he was staying with Gabe while his parents were out of town. The boys got drunk, went up to the school, and broke a bunch of windows. They're suspended for two days and can't run track this season.

"I can't believe it," I say, but this still doesn't explain Dayna's tears. Then she tells me Jamie and Bianca were there too. Even though Gabe and Dayna were going out again, Jamie and Gabe made out. Bianca got together with Cody even though he's going with Linnea. I can't even look at Jamie or Bianca who keep their distance because they know they messed up.

When I get home from school Mom asks what kind of trouble my friends got in. When I tell her about the boys she says, "Well, it's a good thing you were out of town."

The way Mom looks at me I can tell she doesn't trust me.

"I wouldn't have been there, Mom," I say, but she just shakes her head.

The thing is, I don't know what would have happened if I had been in town. Would Dayna and I have been there? Would we have stayed out of trouble or been caught up in this madness?

We have a history test on Friday and all of the boys who are suspended miss it. I write about tensions building up between the North and the South because of Eli Whitney's cotton gin. That's what led to the country's split and the Civil War. I imagine our group of friends splitting because of one night of chaos. I finish my test and lay my head on my desk. I look at Cougar and Gabe's empty seats and thank God March Madness saved me from this mess.

DC

Kim and Bianca are signed up to go on Mrs. McAdams's summer American Heritage summer trip to DC. I asked Mom if I could go and she told me the family was traveling to DC for spring break. It would cost the same for our whole family to go back east as it would to send just me on American Heritage. I said, "Okay, whatever," and then sulked in my room.

Months later, I shove clothes in a bag for spring break. I wish I was going with a friend, but this is a "family vacation." Great. Laura and Mitch will hardly talk to me, and Chet will still think of me as the little kid I was before he left for college. Mom and Dad say they love me but it must be hard when I throw fits and slam doors and tell Mom I hate her. I zip up my bag and imagine I'm packing for a trip like the one Laura took to DC with the marching band or to San Diego with the choir.

We drive to Portland and board the plane, but I don't want anyone to know this is my first flight. I hide my excitement under a façade of cool. I watch the passengers around me who have heard the flight attendants' safety routine and mimic their nonchalance. Mom asks what I think about the plane and I shrug. "It's like a bus that flies." I fasten my seatbelt and look out the window. We're on a red-eye so even though I feel the plane rise from the earth, I can't see a thing. We hurl through space at speeds I've never traveled and while my family and the other passengers sink into their seats and wrap up in blankets, I close my eyes and pretend I fly every day. From inside the plane's noisy darkness I imagine leaving Oregon, heading to Harvard or Georgetown. Behind navy lids, I dream of my escape from this family and our small-town life.

Uncle Min and Auntie Rose's house is on a lake in Maryland about a half-hour outside of DC. It's cold, so the trees around their house are still bare, but I want a tan so badly

I lay out and attempt to summon warmth from the weak sunshine.

We visit the monuments, and Uncle Min, who used to work for NASA, shows us around the Air and Space Museum. We check out Georgetown and drive to Philadelphia where Mom and Dad lived after they got married. It's hard to picture Mom and Dad before us, living in this city with no kids. Laura is actually nice during parts of the trip and it's fun having Chet around. There's some sort of magic with all four of us together. We hang out and tease one another just like old times.

Dad drives along turnpikes and highways, through rain and hail storms all the way to New York City. A few days ago I'd imagined myself going to Georgetown in DC, but the energy of New York City feels like nowhere I've ever been. I start to wonder about Columbia or NYU.

We walk the crowded sidewalks, and I'm in awe of all the people. I get dizzy staring up into smooth, clean glass of skyscrapers climbing into the cloudy sky. In the World Trade Center the rush-hour crowd streams past. I stare at the flow of people. Not one of them pauses or glances in my direction. The city has a pulse with masses in trench coats surging through its veins and arteries. They race through a life so different than mine, but watching them is like staring at the Deschutes River as it flows down the mountain, through our town, and toward the ocean. These people are like that rush of water, speeding past; never stopping.

We take the Staten Island Ferry out of the city and as the city skyline glitters behind us, I hope I'll make it back here. I will get to know some of these millions of people and harness the city's energy. The lights of Manhattan reflect off the water and I hope, wherever life takes me, I'll find my way back to New York City someday.

Turning Fourteen

For my fourteenth birthday I want to have the biggest party ever, and I want it to be coed. Mom tells me to come up with a list and for three days I write down names on a piece of notebook paper. It adds up to over 50 people. Mom figures out how to make it work with Val and Joe's moms. Val's birthday is right before mine and Joe Speck's is right after so we're going to have one big party together, all three of us.

The RSVPs start to come in, but the only one I really care about is Robert. Jackie can't come though, so I doubt Robert will. Jackie has recently become annoyed by our friendship. Still, I hope he might surprise me and show up.

Fifty people have never packed our house before, not even during the holidays when all of Dad's family is in town. The boys hang out in the family room and play ping-pong. Groups of girls hang out all over the house, sit on the couch or the floor, or play the piano. I watch the door for Robert and before I know it, it's time for the cake. Joe, Val, and I pose for pictures while everyone sings "Happy Birthday." We blow out the candles and then the phone rings.

"Hey, Nori, it's Robert."

"Oh, hey." Robert's never called me before. My face goes flush and I press the receiver hard against my ear so I can hear every word he says.

"Sorry I couldn't make it. You know, it's weird with Jackie."

"Yeah, no prob," I say. "Thanks for calling. It means a lot." I hang up and that one call makes my whole night.

Joe, Val, and I help Mom, Mrs. Speck, and Mrs. Segerstrom clean up and before I head up to bed I thank Mom for letting me have a coed party.

I close the door to my bedroom, which is clean for once. I look at my Michael Jordan/Mars Blackmon and INXS posters, the photos of friends plastering my walls, and love that so many people peaked into my life tonight. I hope they saw who I really am. I flip off the light and I crawl into bed. Moonlight shines through the window. Fourteen has to be better than thirteen. Thirteen kinda sucked.

The Waiting Game

A couple of days after the party I hear Robert and Jackie might break-up and the possibility of Robert being single bubbles up inside me. I wonder when I can come clean and finally say I like him.

I'm sitting in Algebra when Val leans over and asks if I heard.

"Heard what?"

"Jackie and Robert just broke up."

I can tell by the smile on Val's face that she isn't telling me because she knows I like him. "Do you like him?" I ask.

"I think so," she says with a smile.

Val and I are friends now so even though I want to tell her I've liked Robert for months I say, "I'll find out if he likes anyone." With that one question I'm stuck waiting again. I move to the back of the room and sit with Robert, DJ, and Issac. I don't say anything at first and hurry through the first set of problems. When I finish, I shake my head annoyed this has happened.

"You okay, Nor?" Robert asks and I look up at him.

"Yeah, yeah. Are you?" I look right at him so he knows I heard about him and Jackie.

"Totally. I'm fine." I'm still playing the friend. Instead of confessing my crush, I let my shot with Robert pass me by. In Mrs. Whitworth's class we've been reading poetry and talking about *carpe diem*, but all I've managed to seize is my role as matchmaker. "So, Robert, I know someone who likes you," I tell him as he finishes the last problem. I wonder if he thinks it's me because the air feels so charged whenever we talk or pass one another in the hall. I look toward the front of the room where Val and Amy Oliver are working.

"Val? Really?" I can tell by his reaction he likes her too.

The next day Robert asks Val out. I pretend to be happy.

Kim passes me a note.

Nor, (The VP)–
Guess what I heard today... Cougar likes Val.
Crazy, huh?
WB Kim

I read Kim's note but all I'm thinking is: seize the day. Val has liked Cougar forever. When she finds out he likes her I bet she'll break up with Robert. In Algebra, Mrs. Pepper graphs parabolas. I have to play this whole Cougar thing right. If I'm too obvious people will think I'm trying to break up Val and Robert. Mrs. Pepper finishes the example on the chalkboard. I haven't been paying attention so it looks like a foreign language. She gives us our assignment and tells us to get to work. We slide chairs and desks together, and as I move next to Val she peers over her shoulder at Robert.

"Will you find out if Robert's mad at me?" she asks as we take out sheets of notebook paper.

"Why?"

She shrugs. "We've hardly talked since we started going out."

There's the crack in their relationship and I wonder how I can wedge my way in without anyone seeing. I look at the first problem and have no idea where to begin. "Why don't you go sit with him?" She shakes her head. "Do you still like him?"

Val glances toward the back of the room. "Yeah, I mean, I guess."

I look over my shoulder to make sure Robert's not looking. "Well, if you aren't sure, I know someone who likes you."

Val looks up at me. I can tell she's curious.

I sit back in my chair and pretend to work. At the end of the period I tell Val to call me tonight.

I drip inside the crack opening up between Val and Robert like water. I just have to wait for their relationship to turn cold. Then the water will freeze, the crack will split them apart, and this time I'll be ready.

Val calls that night and I tell her about Cougar.

"Really? I've liked him forever, but I like Robert too."

I take a deep breath. "I have to tell you something, Val." *Carpe diem.* "I like Robert. I have since basketball season."

"Why didn't you tell me?"

"I don't know."

"Well, I'm glad you did, but I'm confused. I don't know what to do."

I hang up the phone, and I'm afraid to hope. I don't want to be disappointed if things with Robert don't work out.

The next day, I hear Robert's going to break up with Val. Val starts crying in Mrs. Whitworth's class, and I don't get it. I thought she was going to break up with him.

That night I call Val and she tells me they broke up. I tell her I'm sorry, but I'm trying to calculate how long I have to wait before I tell Robert how I feel. I write him a note in my head that explains how sometimes friends become more than friends and how I've been waiting *forever*.

Two days is all I can wait before I seize the day. I don't care what people think. I like Robert and I want to scream it from the top of Pilot Butte for everyone to hear. I can't say it out loud though. Instead I write notes that get passed from friend to friend to friend so fast that by the start of fifth period (when I carefully choreograph walking into math class at the same time as Robert) I'm sure he's heard. He smiles at me, and there is something completely different about the way our eyes meet. My insides feel carbonated, and he let's me walk through the door first.

Mrs. Pepper starts class and through her whole lecture I can feel Robert's gaze behind me. She explains the assignment and as the equations take shape on the chalkboard, I can't wait for her to finish so I can move to Robert's desk to work. When she's done I move across from Robert. DJ, and Isaac don't slide their desks over. It's just Robert and me and suddenly the only thing we have to talk about is math. I'm so nervous I forget what seven times eight is. I stare at Robert's paper as he flies through problems. In sixth grade, when we first met in math class, the problems were so much simpler to solve. Back then I was the new girl, and we were friends. Finally, we can become more. The bell rings and we move the desks back into rows. On the way out of class Robert says, "Hey, Nor, wait up."

I turn and look back at him. He puts his arm around my shoulder and pulls me close. I relax into him.

He asks right in my ear so only I can hear, "So, you wanna go out?"

The sound of his voice gives me goose bumps and the effervescence I've been holding on to for so long explodes. I have to be cool though. I grin up at him and say, "Of course. I thought you'd never ask."

Perfect Couple

Robert calls me that night and we talk for almost an hour. "I can't believe we're finally going out," He says.

I laugh. "No, I can't believe it. I've been waiting forever."

"No," he insists, "I've been waiting since sixth grade when I first saw you throw that football."

We debate whose wait has been harder, but it doesn't matter. Our moment has finally come. We set a date to play basketball after school, a game we've been talking about since sixth grade.

For a few days it doesn't feel real. Robert walks me to class. We hold hands. He drapes his long arm around my shoulders. It's so easy to be with him and he smells good; not like Casey, something cleaner. He smells different than any other boy I've been with and when we finally kiss (outside the choir room before he goes to band and I go to Ensemble) I sink into him. Everyone thinks we're the cutest couple and when I ask why they say we're the best basketball players, but I'm sure it also has to do with me being half-Japanese and him being half-Polynesian. We're practically the only two Asian kids in school.

Every once in a while we talk about the future, how he's going to Bend High and I'm going to Mountain View but we'll stay together. We'll hang out after school and on weekends, go to both schools' homecomings and proms together. Then we'll go to college and play basketball, but I can't see what college that might be. Robert is Mormon. He'll go to Utah, or BYU, or Ricks in Idaho. Then, he'll go on a mission. I'll attend an Ivy League school; board a plane to New York or Boston. That's when I think Robert and I might not work out. Robert tells me not to think so much, to just enjoy the moment. He's right, so I try not to think about the future. I try to enjoy what I've imagined for months. Eighth grade has had its ups and downs, but right now, it's perfect.

Say Goodbye

In Ensemble, Mr. Miller writes a song with a tight four-part harmony.

"The days are growing longer, leaves appear and flowers bloom.
Tell tale signs we'll soon be parting, for our time is over soon.
It's so hard to think that I won't see you when fall colors show
but rather than to say goodbye, let's plan to say hello."

As we rehearse, I get sentimental. So much has changed over three years and I hardly recognize that little girl from St. Francis who started sixth grade not knowing anyone. Now she's student body Vice President, going out with Robert White, singing in Ensemble, and hanging out with the cool kids. Three years spent in careful social studies and decision-making are about to end and high school is next.

I write a graduation speech. Ever since Chet's high school graduation I've wanted to be the valedictorian addressing the class, but at Pilot Butte we aren't allowed to say graduation. This is a promotion. Our teachers want us to think of high school graduation as the real one. I try to write a speech from my heart. I channel Kevin Bacon at the end of *Footloose* and Patrick Swayze before the final dance at Kettleman's in *Dirty Dancing*. I don't want it to be sad or to make anyone cry. I want us to remember all of the good times, go to our last dance, and have the best time ever.

They don't choose my speech. They choose Bianca's. She writes a poem that rhymes.

"Congrats, Bink," I tell her after school. We walk along the irrigation ditch. The water flows past Bianca's house, then past Robin's, and finally past mine. We stand there for a minute and watch the water.

"I wish they could have chosen both of them," Bianca tells me.

I shrug and kick at the gravel. "Your speech really is great."

"Thanks, Nor," she says, and then she reaches over for a one-armed hug. "See you tomorrow."

"Not unless I see you first," I say with a grin and turn to walk the rest of the way home alone.

It's a clear day and from the top of Revere the snow-capped Cascades: Bachelor, Broken Top, and the Three Sisters stand majestic, keeping watch over our town. I walk in silence and think about all the times I walked this way with Robin, and the few times Casey walked me home. I pass Jason's house, and remember that awful New Year's Eve party. I felt so empty on that dark night. But winter's snow and ice have melted and I don't have to walk carefully anymore. Black ice won't send me crashing to the ground. It's spring, and instead of snow and cinders, juniper pollen coats the roadsides. Spring blossoms make way for lush leaves, and I'm happy.

This is not a walk I will take again, so I breathe in the pine needles covering the ground and the sun shining through the ponderosas. I pass the stretch Robin, Jamie, and I call Boner Road because a horse there once had a big, pink boner. Rusty metal "No Trespassing" and "Keep Out" signs hang on the barbed wire fence reminding me of *To Kill A Mockingbird* and the Radley's creaky old porch.

I can see my house and Robin's too. I don't want to tell Mom they didn't choose my speech, but in middle school I've learned heartbreak is temporary. Like the water flowing past Bianca's house, Robin's house, and mine, this disappointment will pass. I hum the song Mr. Miller wrote: "Better than to say goodbye, let's plan to say hello." I still owe Robin an apology, but it's too late. Maybe that's what coming of age is all about. Maybe being an adult means you've done things you aren't proud of, things you can't take back, things you have to live with. I never walk over to Robin's house. I never say goodbye to Robin, so we can't plan to say hello.

Last Summer

Promotion is perfect. My family, even Chet, is there and even though I don't give the graduation speech, they seem proud of me. At the graduation party I dance every fast song with my friends and Robert holds me for every slow song. I spend the night at Jamie's and neither of us can believe it's over. The excitement of the last day bleeds into another summer.

Over those first weeks of summer Jamie and I ride our bikes over to Chris Rexrode's house where all the boys are. We watch *Can't Buy Me Love* over and over again and study how high school girls dress and act. I ride over to Robert's house and a couple of days later he rides over to mine. We hold hands and I lean against him even though Mom is right in the other room. We watch baseball until he has to go home and I wonder how long our perfect relationship can last.

One afternoon, Dayna and Jamie are hanging out and a bunch of boys stop by the house. I find a way to sneak around Mom's "no friends in the house when we're not home" rule and invite everyone up to the sun deck. Even though Robert and I are still going out, Cougar is flirty, and I flirt back. Coug doesn't believe I can take my bra off without taking off my shirt.

"I totally can," I say amazed he doesn't get how it works.

"Fine, show me."

I walked right into that one, but I don't care. "Whatever." I reach under my t-shirt. I stretch my arms behind my back and unhook my bra. I pull one strap over my shoulder and then thread the white, cotton bra out along my left arm. Cougar stares, in awe, and I realize I'm standing in the afternoon sunshine, naked under my t-shirt, with my bra in my hand. I laugh nervously because I hadn't thought about how I would get my bra back on.

I head into the dark of the house to get dressed. I close the bathroom door and think about Robert. What am I going to tell him about this afternoon? It's not like I cheated on him. I didn't kiss Cougar or anything, but I feel dirty even after I wash my hands. I go back outside and tell the boys they should leave. Dayna and Jamie leave with them.

By the time I call Robert I've already decided things aren't going to work out. I'm not good enough for him. He would hate the girl I was this afternoon. Maybe I'm more like Casey and Jen than I thought. I can't be trusted. I don't even trust myself.

"It's just too hard," I tell Robert. I add something about us going to different schools and never seeing one another, but I don't tell him he's too good for me. I tell him I hope we can still be friends and I really mean it. I'm sad when I hang up and wish I could have found the words to tell him how much I still like him. But if we stayed together, I'd only let him down. I hang up the phone and add another secret to my collection: I'm a terrible girlfriend.

Dusk falls in Juniper Park and the silhouettes of pine trees press against the sky. I sit on a picnic table with Jamie, Bianca, and Dayna listening to INXS on Chris Rexrode's CD player. The boys throw around a football and I play "Need You Tonight" over and over again. When Michael Hutchinson whispers, *"Come over here,"* it sounds like he's right in my ear. I can feel his desire.

"All you've got is this moment."

I know what he means. *Carpe diem.* These are the last moments we will all share. In high school everything will change.

"You can care all you want, everybody does yeah, that's okay."

I know I care. Gabe has told me I care too much about what other people think.

"How do you feel?"

"I'm lonely."

I'm lonely, even with friends around, and I'm lonelier at home.

"What do you think?"

"Can't think at all."

I don't want to think about any of it, about eighth grade ending, breaking up with Robert, Gabe's sister dying, the way we cast Robin out, Laura crying at night, or Chet hearing voices in his head. I want to ignore the kind of person I've turned out to be. I thought I knew who I was, but my choices haven't been the right ones. That Robert Frost poem haunts me. I can't stop picturing those two roads in a yellow wood.

"Whatchya gonna do?"

"Gonna live my life."

What else can I do, but keep living? It's not like I want to kill myself, even though I have thought about it. I've thought about it more than I'm supposed to, like every time we cross the Crooked River Gorge. I wish I knew the right road to take. I know that would make all the difference.

The sun is setting. I'm supposed to be home. I give Chris his CD player and climb on my bike. As the silhouettes of my friends fade away with the summer light, I ride home alone.

Unbridgeable Gap

Jamie's still my best friend but we're drifting apart. She is obsessed with Gabe even though he tells me she has to stop calling. One afternoon I ride to her house and she's in the bathroom with the door closed.

"What's going on?" I ask from one side of the door.

She laughs as she flings the door open, runs into her room and sloshes onto the waterbed. "Um, you aren't going to believe what I just did." She flips her head over and I can see, under her thick, blonde hair, a strip shaved clean.

"Why, Jaym?" I ask but she doesn't answer. She won't make eye contact, and I feel her slipping away from me. We used to tell one another everything, but I haven't told her how a light went out inside me when Casey cheated on me, or the real reason I broke up with Robert. I wonder what she hasn't told me, what might be happening behind those green eyes to make her shave away her beautiful, blonde hair.

I start hanging out more with Dayna and Kim and when Gabe and Jason invite us to the reservoir for their birthday, Jamie's not included. Kim, Dayna, and I head up to the lake with Gabe, Cody, Jason, and their families. Along the dusty shore of Lake Billy Chinook, Cody's dad loads us into the boat. Gabe and Jason's moms hang out in the shade. As we pull away and they wave, and I wave back. The boat skims over smooth navy water, and I wonder what those moms are thinking. What will they talk about as we speed across the water? Does Gabe's mom think of Wendy as she watches us splashing along the shore? Does Jason's mom, who has cancer, imagine the birthdays to come she might miss?

The boat gains speed and the wind whips through my hair. I watch Gabe and Jason jump the wake on their kneeboards and when we pull back into shore, the moms are nothing but smiles. They serve us lunch and birthday cake and as the guys blow out the candles I smile and forget my little-girl problems. If Gabe and Jason's moms can soak up this bright blue summer day with all they've been through, I can too. Even though Jamie and I are drifting apart, even though my family doesn't like me, even though I'm not the kind of person I want to be, it's a beautiful day on the lake. It's okay for me to be happy.

On a morning when the cool of fall replaces the heat of summer Kim, Bianca, and I walk through the mall. Bright light reflects off the shiny tile, but something doesn't feel right. Jamie is in Portland for Labor Day weekend but she should be here with us. We're about to start high school and we should be heading there together. She's gone, though, and as we walk past K-Mart, Orange Julius, and the movie theatre, I wonder if this is how it will be from now on. With the gap widening between Jamie and I, will it just be Bianca, Kim and me, sometimes Dayna? Will we move on just like we did with Robin, never mentioning her again? Someday will it be me? Will I leave the fold of these friendships too? We window shop, and talk about the first day of school, but for most of the afternoon, I have nothing to say.

On the day before school starts Jamie comes home and when she calls I'm nervous. I'm not sure why, but I'm anxious to talk with her. I've been measuring the growing distance between us, trying to figure out how to bridge the gap in our friendship. I hope she'll open up, say something that will help bring us together. It's only been a year, but the day before eighth grade seems like forever ago. Jamie and I rode our bikes to Taco Bell and we laid out on the Bend sign. We were so close. Now we're about to start high school and I have no idea what's happening. I ask her about Portland but she doesn't have much to say.

"Is everything okay?"

"Yeah, of course," she says but I don't believe her.

Can she feel the expanse opening between us? I felt so alone after Casey and I broke up that second time. I hid how hurt I was and how the whole world looked different. A light went out inside me but no one could see it. I wonder if the same thing has happened to Jamie and I never noticed. "Come on, Jaym," I don't want her to hide from me. I want her to talk to me. "You can tell me anything."

"Really, everything's fine. Why? Are you okay?" she asks.

I don't answer. I sit there, with the long phone cord stretched across the kitchen, swaying back and forth. A tense silence builds and even though I want to tell her it's going to be okay, that we're best friends and I'll be there no matter what, I know it's not true. The silence grows and like a river carving away at the land year after year, a gorge grows deeper and wider. Jamie stands on one side and I'm on the other. I wait for her to say something. I play with the long yellow telephone cord, make it bounce up and down on the parquet floor as the river erodes our friendship. It started with small secrets and little lies but has grown wider and now the expanse is unbridgeable. The Crooked River Gorge has opened up between us. If I try to jump across I will fall into empty space.

With nothing to say, Jamie and I hang up. I don't cry about losing my best friend. I don't feel anything. I hover in the empty expanse between us and wait to fall.

Set Adrift

On my first day of high school I head to Mountain View where Chet, Laura, and Mitch have all left their mark. Chet is at the University of Hawaii for the year. Laura is at Western Oregon where she'll play basketball. Mom takes classes at the community college and Dad keeps waking up and heading to the Forest Service where he's worked as long as I've been alive. We survived Chet's breakdown, Laura's tears at night, and months of marriage counseling. Mitch runs cross-country and I immerse myself in volleyball, school, and new friendships. Our family carries on.

On the other side of town, Robert, Casey, and Jen make their way to Bend High and we lose touch. Bianca, Kim, Jamie, Dayna, and I sit in the freshman commons. We take in this new world, but we rarely look at one another. Middle school was simple, but in high school we start to hang out with boys who drive and go to parties with booze, drugs, and sex behind closed doors. Kim dates a senior and the Westside boys ask us to homecoming before Gabe, Jason, and Cody think about dates. I stop talking to the boys I was so close to at Pilot Butte. In the chaos of this new world my secrets fade away. The apologies I owe slip from memory. But Bend is a small town and reminders of the past constantly resurface.

Robin and her mom pull out of their driveway across the street and I wave. Robin doesn't see me, or she isn't interested in waving back. I never call. I never walk across the street to make amends.

Gabe watches me play volleyball and basketball; I watch his football games, but when we see one another in class, at dances, or parties we don't talk. We don't share our dreams anymore. I never tell him I'm sorry about his sister. I never say I regret missing the funeral; that I wish we were still friends.

I pass Jamie everyday. We make eye contact and smile. We know so much about one another, but with each day there is more we haven't talked about. Like at the end of *Stand By Me*, friends become like busboys in a restaurant. Jamie becomes another face in the hall and in the silence separating us I never tell her I'm sorry we never found a bridge to sustain our friendship.

I see Robert at Sadie Hawkins and my stomach churns. I watch his basketball games and can predict his every move. I watch him from a distance, but never tell him I'm sorry for breaking up when I still liked him. I never tell him I didn't trust myself, that he was too good for me.

Time moves slowly in Bend, the same way the Deschutes River flows through town. At Mirror Pond, I stare at my reflection, but that girl is a stranger. The water looks still, but it carves away at the land and the current can carry you away. I drift through the days and nights and although Jamie, Bianca, Dayna, and Kim float with me for a while, we eventually catch different currents and float in different directions. I look downstream for a rapid to carry me away.

I wish I could go back, still the current of this river, row against the tide, paddle upstream and do things differently. I shiver at all the apologies I owe and wonder if anyone holds an apology for me. That's what growing up is about. It's the collection of mistakes and regrets that become part of you. Alongside all you are proud of, all you want to be, is all that shames you.

I breathe in Bend's wet juniper and pine, stony water and dry air. The Deschutes flows from the mountain, slips around boulders and obsidian slats, narrows into rapids, and gathers in swirls and eddies.

I don't have the words to form the apologies to help me sleep better at night, but maybe the words I'm sorry aren't as important as learning how to forgive. Maybe, someday, I'll let go of my overdue apologies. Maybe, with time, I'll let them all wash away.

thank you...

to Bend, for a providing a beautiful backdrop for growing up.

to my family, for letting me write about them once again.

to my middle school friends, for sharing so many intimate moments of our youth, for reading early drafts, and supporting this project.

to my students, for reminding me what middle school is like every single school day.

to Hazel and Randy, for reading early drafts and helping me craft this story.

and to David, for helping me forgive the girl I was in middle school.

Made in the USA
Lexington, KY
04 April 2012